Willard Scott's
All-American
☆ Cookbook ☆

Also by Willard Scott

The Joy of Living
Down Home Stories

Willard Scott's All-American ☆ Cookbook ☆

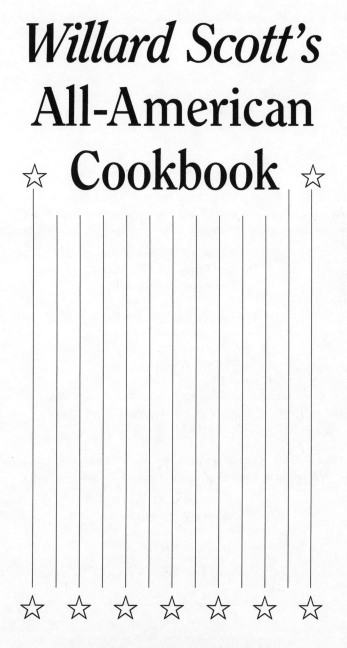

Macmillan Publishing Company

New York

Macmillan Publishing Company
866 Third Avenue, New York, N.Y. 10022
Collier Macmillan Canada, Inc.

Library of Congress Cataloging-in-Publication Data
Scott, Willard.
Willard Scott's all-American cookbook.
Includes index.
1. Cookery, American.   I. Title.   II. Title: All-
American cookbook.   III. Title: All-American cook book.
TX715.S4326   1986   641.5973   86-12864
ISBN 0-02-608800-2

Macmillan books are available at special discounts for bulk purchases for sales promotions,
premiums, fund-raising, or educational use. For details, contact:

Special Sales Director
Macmillan Publishing Company
866 Third Avenue
New York, New York 10022

10   9   8   7   6   5   4   3   2   1

Designed by Mary Cregan

Printed in the United States of America

☆ ☆ ☆

Contents

☆　☆　☆

Acknowledgments

This book would not have been possible without the willingness which so many great restaurants around the country have shown in sharing their cooking secrets with us. I've had some of the most satisfying times of my life at the fantastic eating establishments mentioned throughout this book. I trust that you'll be able to say the same as you cook some of the same dishes in the privacy of your own home.

I also want to thank my friend and collaborator William Proctor for helping me put this book together. His editorial skills have proved invaluable, as have those of his associates, Kim Flowers, Janet Ernst, and Fafa Demasio.

Willard Scott's
All-American
☆ Cookbook ☆

☆ 1 ☆

An Experienced Eater's Philosophy of Food

There's an old expression, "He was born with a silver spoon in his mouth." But that's not me. I was born with a *soup* spoon in mine—and there was still plenty of room for a knife, a fork, *and* a ladle!

Eating was almost a religious experience in our family.

My dad, Herman, was a big eater. He would inhale anything that was put in front of him. My mom, Thelma, also had a love affair with food. Of course, she prepared the food in our family. So she was the one who was responsible for the quality, tastes, and tantalizing aromas in our household.

Eating in the great Scott tradition is an activity with roots that run deep into the past. In fact, I think that our near-obsession with fine, flavorful foods may be hereditary.

I suppose every family has its apocryphal stories and fond memories that suggest something about the innate character of one's ancestral lineage. I'm sure, for example, there must have been a Lord Willard who stocked the cellar of his medieval manor with slabs of beef, pounds of poultry, stalks upon stalks of the tastiest veggies, and, of course, every conceivable variety of sweets.

My own earliest recollections center on rollicking repasts at my grandparents' farm in Maryland. Ironically, many of those memories go back to the early days of the Second World War, when food rationing was in effect. That was a sad time for anyone with a big appetite. You had to get stamps from the government to buy meat, sugar, bread, or practically anything else that was worth eating.

But we Scotts had a major advantage. My grandparents grew much of their own food, so when it came time to go to Grandmother's house,

3

the term "food rationing" lost its meaning, because most of the food on the table came from the garden or the barnyard, not from a store. About the only things from a store that went into our stomachs were coffee, salt, and B.C. Headache Powder!

Grandma always set incredible amounts of food before us: Huge platters of fried chicken, biscuits, rolls, gravy, beans, beets, pies, cakes—you name it, we savored it!

Of course, because farm people did more physical work than most of us today, they burned off all those extra calories. They ate three meals just like we do, but unlike many city folks, they started off with a big breakfast and then consumed a *huge* lunch, which they called "dinner." That was their major meal of the day. The evening snack, which they dubbed "supper," was often made up of the leftovers from dinner.

It's interesting to me that many nutritionists and preventive health specialists have finally "discovered" the health benefits of this old-time approach to distributing calories. There's a growing trend for them to recommend big breakfasts and lunches and small suppers.

It was at the midday "dinner" gatherings that I really came into my own as an eater. I was always big; in fact, by the time I was a teenager, I was the largest person in the family. And when you're big, people tend to give you twice as much food to eat as anyone else. They even get offended if you don't have seconds, thirds, or more!

I've enjoyed this special big-person status all my life. Even my own wife Mary will tell me out of one side of her mouth that I've got to go on a diet. But, when she serves up my plate, there's twice as much food on it as on anyone else's.

My position as an overweight person put pressure on me quite early to develop a personal philosophy of food. If I do say so, I'm one of the greatest living authorities on how to enjoy a good meal. So now, let me give you an overview of the Willard Scott way to supremely joyful health, fitness, and nutrition.

First of all, you've got to come to grips with certain related matters —such as exercise. To put it bluntly, when I go to an exercise club these days, I don't even pretend to exercise anymore. All I do now is enjoy the steam bath.

You see, I learned early on that I hate the stationary bicycle. I'd sit on it and agonize for thirty minutes, pedaling my heart out. But I'd get so bored my eyes would roll back in my head; I couldn't wait for the bell to signal it was time for me to stop. I mean, I'd *live* for that bell to ring!

I still go to the club because I like the atmosphere. But I only do what

I like to do: That means taking my steam bath for half an hour, and then lying down on one of their nice, big lounge chairs to recuperate. Finally, I'll go downstairs to the Friar's Club, which is in the same building. Then, I'll have a bowl of their black bean soup and a salad and talk to some of the guys at one of the tables before I walk home.

I get forty-five minutes of good, healthy exercise on that walk home —and that's exactly the kind of "workout" I like and need. Everybody seems to agree that walking is one of the best exercises of all time. As for me, I've gotten my cue from my idol Harry Truman, who regularly took his "constitutional," a brisk and steady walk for forty-five minutes to one hour each day.

The second principle I follow in my fitness program is that I always have dessert. Probably, by the time we get well into the twenty-first century, we'll have established such perfect eating habits and good nutrition that desserts will be "gone with the wind." But I hope and pray to God I never live to see that day. I simply don't want to live without a sweet, creamy touch to my meals.

Think about it for a minute: Suppose you die and you're put in this nice, roomy six- by four-foot box in the ground. You could lie there for thousands of years before the Last Judgment; and all that time, nobody's going to offer you a chocolate chip cookie. No caramels, no banana pudding. I think that's tragic!

Sweets are something that should be enjoyed all our lives. Remember how excited you got when you heard the bells on the Good Humor truck when you were just a kid? Well, I've got news for you: I know from my own extensive adult experience that Good Humors, and especially orange cream "sickles," still taste as good as they used to. The only big improvement in this kind of sweet is Dove Bars. In my opinion, they are Good Humors that have died and gone to heaven!

No matter how old or young you may be, *now* is the time to enjoy these nice, tasty things that have been given to us—now, while we're *alive.* I ask you: Unless you have a medical problem, is there really any sin in a dessert? We've been made to feel guilty about enjoying sweets, but I've come to terms with that. I just refuse to feel guilty anymore.

So what impact does this philosophy of fitness and nutrition have on my waistline?

I must say that I really envy people who can pack it away and stay nice and thin. We all know people who just eat and eat, but never seem to gain any weight. I'm not one of those people, as you can plainly see if you've ever watched me on television, and I've come to accept that about

5

myself. I made up my mind long ago to buy clothes just a little bigger than I need so that I can be more comfortable as I move about and sit down—but I'm not going to give up my desserts!

Now, let's move from some of these profound philosophical generalizations to concrete, succulent, aromatic, and even gooey reality.

The best place to begin is breakfast. Breakfast is probably my favorite meal. But, in the interest of putting the brakes on my expanding waistline and also my burgeoning clothes budget, I've cut down to one big breakfast a week. The event usually occurs on Saturday or Sunday, and that meal is *really* huge.

The perfect "Willard breakfast" starts off with some fresh apple juice. We squeeze our own apples at home and make the juice that way. Then I move on to grits, ham, sausage, and bacon. By the way, sometimes I'll eat just one of those meats, but at other times, I'll have all three.

The best breakfasts will always include real homemade biscuits and some fried or shirred eggs. I also like to throw in some fried apples and fried potatoes.

Then, there's the coffee. Let me say right now, right up front, that I think instant coffee is an affront to civilization. In fact, it's really an impossible concept, like airline food.

The only time I ever talk back to the TV set is when they put on one of those commercials where some people are in a restaurant and they sneak in and replace real, freshly brewed coffee with the instant variety. Have you seen those ads? They drive me crazy! I don't think anybody who really understands and appreciates real coffee could possibly be fooled by a cup of instant.

Butter is another big issue with me. I'd *never* substitute margarine for real butter. I'm of the school that says, "Butter is what margarine would like to be."

Of course, in this "perfect breakfast," you can always throw in some real-food substitute. Like omelets. I love eggs, so I'll sometimes include them as the main dish. Also, hotcakes and waffles really turn me on.

During the other days of the week, as I'm gathering my energies to attack and savor this super weekend breakfast, I try to exercise some restraint, though this is another form of "exercise" that can give me some trouble. Still, I'll usually stick to fruit for breakfast and a relatively light lunch. If I didn't, I'd soon be bigger than an elephant.

Another practical element in my eating philosophy is variety. I've been to about four hundred American cities in my career, and I've had great food in every one of them. The other day I was trying to figure out how many restaurants I've eaten in. The number I came up with was

Whether it's pork or beef, minced or sliced—a barbecue is always an American favorite. (Photo courtesy of C. Lamberti/WHO Broadcasting)

about five thousand. And the exquisite cooking I've encountered in my travels has really opened my eyes and my taste buds to the possibilities of American cuisine.

We may talk about the finest wine districts of France or the unique foods of Eastern Europe and the Orient, but there's no question in my mind that the tastiest dishes are to be found here in the good old United States.

In part, the potential for eating great food in this country is a result of the diversified European, African, Oriental, and Spanish–Hispanic backgrounds of our American people. But even when you give full credit to the foreign influence, we always seem able to put our own special American twist on every appetizer, entrée, and dessert. The more you sample similar dishes in the different regions of the country, the more you begin to sense the possibilities of the great American smorgasbord.

Take barbecue, for example. When you're in North Carolina, pit-cooked, minced barbecue is the thing. That's barbecue that's all chopped up and served with coleslaw and hot sauce on a bun.

In Memphis, on the other hand, you get sliced barbecue—a nice, neat

7

piece cut right off a side of pork. But in Memphis the sliced barbecue is dry-cooked, while in Little Rock, Arkansas, it's served with barbecue sauce dripping off the sides. (Personally, I prefer it this way.)

What's more, for a Deep-South purist the *only* barbecue is pork. In fact, they believe barbecue is synonymous with pork. Beef barbecue, which is so popular in Texas and other parts of the Southwest, is regarded as something of an aberration by pork aficionados.

I first learned this while visiting Memphis for the National Barbecue Competition a few years ago. This event, which has to be the ultimate barbecue cookout in the entire world, is held annually in Lee Park, just off Mud Island on the banks of the Mississippi River.

There's often something about the special style of cooking barbecue or any other dish, that somehow fits in perfectly with a specific locale. When I was in Little Rock one time, I was invited to a television station party on a beautiful seventy-foot yacht on the Arkansas River. The "runny," juicy Arkansas barbecue I ate at that party actually lays claim to certain national and even international culinary connections, because the port at Little Rock is linked through canals to Tulsa, Oklahoma, as well as to the Gulf of Mexico. In other words, both Tulsa and Little Rock are inland ports, something I didn't realize until I began to sample that tasty Arkansas barbecue.

So experiencing a variety of dishes is important to give you some perspective on life in general. And it's also important to give your taste buds an opportunity to expand and evolve. I believe that if you eat a lot of things and meditate periodically on your reactions to them, you'll find that your taste buds will begin to sharpen.

As a youngster, for instance, I didn't particularly like vegetables. But as I got older, I began to like them more and more, and now I absolutely adore all vegetable dishes. Four types of greens turn me on in a special way: lettuce, kale, turnips, and collards touched up with fatback.

But my favorite of all time is zucchini: I call it King Zucchini, I'm so crazy about it. As far as I'm concerned, it's the "El Supremo" of all vegetables.

Because I take an open-ended approach to food, I've found, over the years, that I like almost anything I put into my mouth. That even includes okra. A lot of people don't like this old Southern vegetable, mainly because it's often served in such a slimy mess. But I learned to like it in Campbell's soup, even though I first tried it I didn't know what it was. Since then, I've learned to go for okra in almost any form, slimy, fried, or whatever.

In more recent years, I've developed a love affair with hot Mexican food, Japanese sushi (raw fish), and even rather exotic offerings such as American "mountain oysters"—bull testicles. (You can't believe how good they can be!)

The one thing I don't like, though, is fishy-smelling fish. I love every kind of fresh fish and other types of seafood, but I'm not real crazy about sardines and other strong-smelling fish dishes. Also, liver isn't my favorite, though I do love pâté. But outside of these few exceptions, I can say, to paraphrase Will Rogers, "I've never met a meal I didn't like."

So when I sit down to eat, I try to savor every second of the experience. That's an important part of my personal philosophy of eating. To enjoy each morsel to the utmost, I've developed a special, "Scott style" of eating. Specifically, there are five ingredients that make this style work for me, and I trust that you may find them helpful as well.

Ingredient #1: Volume eating

I'm not one of those people who will spear a tiny morsel of food on a fork, toy with it, contemplate it for several seconds, and then slowly raise it to my mouth and chew it fifty times. No, I'm a *volume* eater. I eat like a guy on a construction job. I perform a real demolition derby on any dish that's placed in front of me.

So I'll put a piece of meat into my mouth, then some salad, then a little potato, and, finally, maybe some other vegetable. Then, I'll munch and savor them all together, almost getting "high" on all those flavors that are rolling around, titillating my taste buds.

But this is not to say that I advocate bad manners. Quite the contrary, as you can see from the next ingredient.

Ingredient #2: Good manners.

I've always been big on good table manners, probably because my mother was always quoting Emily Post at the dinner table. Also, my father was always saying, "Willard, sit up straight. . . . Get your arms off the table. . . . Quit talking with your mouth full. . . ."

So when I say I'm a volume eater and like to put all sorts of foods into my mouth at the same time, I'm not advocating that people become slobs at mealtime. One of the worst things you can see at a restaurant is a well-dressed, well-groomed person who has atrocious table manners.

Just the other day I was eating at a posh New York restaurant. After glancing over at some people at a nearby table, I mentioned to my companion, "Gee, that's an attractive lady over there." Almost as if on cue, she proceeded to grab her knife and fork in her fists and she went after her salad as though she was ready to introduce *Rambo III*. That's all you have to do to shatter a good impression.

Ingredient #3: A Quick Cleanup.

One thing can really dampen the enthusiasm of a host and hostess, especially during that all-important dessert and coffee phase: That's the thought that there's a stack of dirty dishes waiting to be cleaned.

For this reason, I always think that everybody at an ordinary family meal or informal dinner should pick up a plate or two when he finishes and carry them into the kitchen. If you have a chance, it's also a good idea to scrape the dishes off and clean them up. There should always be more than one set of hands cleaning up the dishes and utensils in the kitchen.

One technique that I've always found to be quite helpful when I'm doing the cooking is to clean as I cook. As soon as I finish using a pot, pan, or dish, I wash it off. As a result, I usually end up with only a couple of dirty pots and pans to wash after the meal.

I can really get into the swing of being efficient in the kitchen. For example, while I'm waiting for the grease to get hot enough to cook some pork chops, I'll automatically begin to clean up the mess I made peeling the potatoes and apples, or whatever.

The entire process of putting together a meal fascinates me so much that I've even thought I might enjoy being a short-order cook someday, with my own bed-and-breakfast place. I'm not sure how long I'd last as a full-time cook, but I certainly can get enthusiastic when I'm cooking for myself a few times a week. And at least part of my enthusiasm for meal-making arises from the fact that I know I've got a relatively clean kitchen to go to when we all get up from the table after that last sip of coffee.

Ingredient #4: No Outside Distractions.

When I eat, I like to concentrate on my food and nothing else. Under no circumstances will I read or watch television when I'm eating. That's an unacceptable distraction from the main event.

In fact, carrying on any other activity at the dinner table is as offensive to me as being in the presence of a woman wearing too much perfume when you open a six-hundred-dollar bottle of wine. Not only are you unable to smell the bouquet of the wine, it doesn't even taste right with all those extraneous scents wafting about!

Perhaps the most offensive distraction to me is television. That may seem a strange notion from someone who makes his living on the tube, but, in part, my attitude is based on a personal need to have a peaceful atmosphere at the dinner table. I see the dinnertime experience as a somewhat sacred event. So I really like to concentrate on my food when it's put before me.

I might take a little slice of pork onto my fork, run it through some mashed potatoes, and then dip it into a little bit of greens. Finally, I'll inhale that delicious mixture of aromas and pop the morsel into my mouth—and, as often as not, at that very moment I'll look out the window and think I'm about to be transported to heaven!

I don't mean to be sacrilegious, but to me, a good meal is just another illustration of that phrase we use in church during communion, "the gifts of God for the people of God."

There are only a few unadorned, lasting pleasures in life and they're usually quite simple: things like your love for your spouse; the joy of holding your baby in your arms; and, of course, the pleasure of enjoying a good, home-cooked meal.

In its purest form, eating should be a spiritual experience. For me, it all begins when I'm working in my garden, making things grow. I get involved in harvesting them, scrubbing them up, preparing and cooking them, and finally eating them. When you participate in this process, you're performing an ancient ritual, a lovely, deeply-satisfying act that I refuse to spoil with outside distractions.

Ingredient #5: Togetherness at Mealtime.

Whenever possible, I try to take my meals with my family or some friends. I don't think it's essential to have every meal at home like the Norman Rockwell painting of the family sitting around an old-fashioned dinner table. But at least one meal a day with others whom you love and respect is almost essential for maintaining a sound mind.

Of course, sometimes my odd hours and extensive travel do require that I eat by myself. On those occasions, I'll often go to a restaurant where I know the waiters or the owner. That makes me feel more comfortable and secure. The waiter, the cook, or the owner will usually come over and chat for a while, and that can be quite pleasant. But, generally speaking, eating alone is a poor substitute for a meal with others.

Inevitably, when I'm alone, I'll be a little on edge. As I'm sitting by myself, for instance, I may sense that somebody who has seen me on television is staring. No matter how long you've been in the public eye, this sort of attention can make you feel a little self-conscious. More often than not, I'll drop a piece of lettuce on the floor or splatter some food in the plate and get oil or sauce on my tie. It's hard to relax in such a situation: Performers and TV personalities always feel a little like they're on stage when they're in a public place. And that feeling can be magnified for me if I'm off in a corner eating by myself.

So I'm a big advocate of togetherness at mealtime. Good food calls for a celebration, and it's hard to celebrate when you're trying to be an "island unto yourself."

★

Finally, one of the most important parts of my personal philosophy of eating involves the natural touch. As far as I'm concerned, nothing tastes quite as good as a potato freshly dug out of the ground, or a crisp ear of corn just off the stalk. The same holds true for meat, fruit, or any other type of food. There's just no comparison between a vine-ripened tomato and one that's been sitting in a store for days or weeks.

On occasion I've said I'll eat anything you put in front of me, but I have some definite preferences. As far as I'm concerned, the fresher and more natural a meal is, the better.

Clearly, for me, food is an affair of the heart. Other guys devote their lives to women—I prefer food.

But now, let's move from the philosophical to the practical. Good food, after all, isn't something you merely *think* about: It's something that tantalizes, seduces, inspires, evokes ecstasy—and always satisfies. To see just how this happens, all you have to do is read on.

Just Desserts

I'm a dessert-a-holic, and I make no bones about it.

When it comes to sweets, apologies and guilt feelings are for other people. Puddings, cakes, and candies are just part of my personality: I came to accept this fact about myself long ago.

In fact, I can't remember when I didn't like sweets. I'm sure when I was just an infant I chose the banana and chocolate pablum and turned up my nose at the creamed peas and spinach.

My favorite dessert has always been banana pudding with vanilla wafers. It's a simple dish, but one which I originally came to love when I was just a kid eating over at my Aunt Avis' place down in North Carolina. I'll never forget walking into her home, with the smell of pine trees coming in through the windows, and maybe a little heaviness in the air from a recent rain. Then, all those scents would get mixed up with the banana pudding she had just made for dessert.

You may think it's a little strange that I'm starting this cookbook with a chapter on desserts, but if you think about it, it's the most logical thing imaginable. Desserts, after all, are the crowning glory of all food.

Not only that, desserts aren't supposed to be available only after a meal. As a matter of fact, just before composing these very words, I sat down and ate an entire box of chocolate chip cookies—and here it is the middle of the afternoon! Or, if for some reason I haven't had any dessert after my evening meal, I may go to the cupboard and find something a little sweet just before I go to bed. So desserts are for any time, any place, depending upon how they strike your fancy.

It isn't just my idea to lead off a meal or menu with sweets. Consider your average chichi or not-so-chichi restaurant. When you walk through the door and head for your table, what do you often walk past first? Why, the dessert cart, of course!

How many people reading this book have sometimes said to themselves when they enter such an establishment, "I think I'd just like to have the dessert and forget the dinner."

I say, "Why not?" Go ahead and eat that dessert first!

If you take my advice, you'll have plenty of good company. Remember the old tradition of teatime, which still is popular in England and even has its place in some of the finest eating spots in this country. I always like to pop in to the Plaza Hotel in New York for tea during the Christmas season. That way, I can order a cup of tea and a bunch of cookies just before dinner and enjoy the snack while listening to a violin. Teatime is certainly in the best tradition of this dessert-first idea.

I'm even toying with the idea of embarking on a dessert-first *diet*. After all, if you gorge a little on sweets before dinner, it will cut your appetite. My mother, like a lot of others, always said: "Willard, don't eat all that stuff—it's going to spoil your appetite for dinner!"

But again, I say, "Why not?" As long as you succeed in cutting your total calories without completely unbalancing your nutrition, I think that a dessert-first diet concept may be the wave of the future!

Of course, it could be easy to go off the deep end with this dessert-first philosophy, so let me pull back a little. I'll admit that even though I frequently do eat my sweets just before the main meal or at other odd times, I try to pursue my splurging with some moderation.

For example, I've recently started *sharing* desserts. When dining with a friend, I may order a piece of cake and then slice it in two so each of us can eat half. That means only half the calories, but enough sugar to satisfy our needs.

Or sometimes at home, I'll make an apple pie without the crust. I love apple pie so much that I can't do without it. So I'll just go for *part* of it. I'll make the pie filling with plenty of apples and some sugar, butter, and cinnamon, but I won't pour the filling into a crust; I'll just bake it in a pie pan.

What all this comes down to is a frank admission of the Scott way of life: I know I could never completely cut out desserts. So I just have to find my own special ways of enjoying them without totally going overboard and turning into a blimp.

And what an array of possibilities there are for satisfying even the most demanding sweet tooth! The following recipes are some of the highlights of my years of travels around America.

On a scale of one to ten, I would rate The Wigwam Resort in Litchfield Park, Arizona, an *eleven*. It's one of the finest places I've ever been in my life for a family vacation and has probably had as much influence on the Scott family as any spot outside of our own home. In fact, our elder daughter, Mary, fell in love with The Wigwam and also with Arizona when she was only about seven years old. She ended up loving the area so much that she decided to go to school at the University of Arizona, and eventually she met her husband-to-be in Tucson.

The Wigwam is located out in the Arizona desert, in a setting that provides the big sky and wide-open spaces that only the American West can offer.

After you feast on the scenery, there's the food. After a day of horseback riding or other outdoor activity, you can take your meals in a beautiful formal dining room. Or, if you prefer, you can choose the dude ranch cookout, with sizzling steaks over smoking mesquite wood.

Then, you top it all off with one of their great desserts, like this one that The Wigwam's general manager, Clark D. Corbett gave me:

☆ Wigwam Peanut Butter-Cream Pie ☆

2 cups milk
½ teaspoon salt
¼ cup (½ stick) butter
⅓ cup sugar
4 tablespoons cornstarch
½ cup cold water
3 large egg yolks, beaten

3 tablespoons creamy peanut butter
Baked 9-inch pie shell
Whipped cream or meringue for garnish
Chopped salted peanuts for garnish

Bring the milk, salt, butter, and sugar to a boil in a saucepan. Mix the cornstarch with the water; when all the lumps have dissolved, mix in the egg yolks. Pour into the boiling milk mixture. Remove the pan from the heat and whisk until thick and smooth. Now, whisk in the peanut butter. Cool the filling to room temperature; then pour it into the pie shell. Cover and refrigerate until cold; then top with whipped cream or meringue and sprinkle with chopped salted peanuts.
Makes 6 to 8 servings.

★

I can honestly say that as I've traveled around the country I've never encountered a place I didn't like. Every state, city, town, and village has something unique to offer. But when I was asked to give a speech for an education association in Bismarck, North Dakota, I wasn't quite sure what to expect.

I had this vague image of North Dakota which was hard to associate with anything that I had known before. As my plane descended into Bismarck, however, the distinctive, stark beauty of those plains, which stretch out endlessly toward the horizon, hit me with their full, spectacular power.

There aren't a lot of trees up in Bismarck, but there's an awful lot of sunlight—more than in any other city in the United States, according to national weather statistics. Of course, during the winter it may get down to 40 degrees below zero, with the wind sometimes blowing at near-gale force. But the winds are one of the reasons for the sunlight: They blow all those clouds away!

Sure enough, it was as bright and sunny as any place I've ever seen when I arrived there for my speech. The mayor of Bismarck, an Irish–American from Chicago, met me at the plane in a stagecoach—now that was style!

One of the first things that my host did was to whisk me into The Gourmet House Restaurant in Bismarck. The hostess who met me at the door said, "I know you're from the South. But if you think you've got pecan pie down there, I want you to taste some of ours!"

And I must say, that was one of the best pecan pies I've ever had in my life. I ranted and raved so much about it that the cook fixed an extra one for me to take home.

Unfortunately, though, I wasn't going directly home. I was scheduled to do the *Phil Donahue Show* in Chicago the next day. But I wasn't about to leave that pecan pie behind, so I put it into my briefcase and took it with me to Chicago. I was so attached to that dessert that I even took it with me on the set for the Donahue program!

Phil couldn't resist it either, and so we sat there in front of millions of viewers, munching away on that Gourmet House Southern Pecan Pie. Here's the recipe so that you can try some yourself. I've also decided to throw in their Cream Cheese Cheesecake as an additional treat.

☆ Southern Pecan Pie ☆

½ cup (1 stick) butter
¾ cup packed dark brown sugar
4 large eggs, slightly beaten
1 cup dark corn syrup
1½ cups whole pecan halves

½ teaspoon salt
1 teaspoon vanilla extract
Unbaked 9-inch pie shell
Pecan halves and whipped cream
 for garnish

Preheat the oven to 450 degrees. Cream the butter and sugar together. Add the eggs and blend well; then stir in syrup, pecans, salt, and vanilla. Turn into the prepared pastry and bake for 10 minutes. Lower the oven temperature to 350 degrees and bake about 30 minutes longer, or until a knife inserted near the center comes out clean. Garnish with additional pecan halves and serve with whipped cream, if desired.
Makes 6 to 8 servings.

☆ Cream Cheese Cheesecake ☆

FILLING
6 8-ounce packages cream
 cheese, softened
1½ cups sugar
Grated rind of ½ lemon
Juice of ½ lemon
6 large eggs, well beaten
2 tablespoons Cognac

CRUST
1¼ cups graham cracker crumbs
¼ cup (½ stick) butter, melted
¼ cup plus 2 tablespoons sugar
2 cups (1 pint) sour cream
Blanched almonds and fruit
 topping to taste

Preheat the oven to 350 degrees. Beat the cream cheese with an electric mixer for 5 minutes. Slowly add the sugar, lemon rind, lemon juice, eggs, and Cognac. Mix well.

To make the crust, mix together the graham cracker crumbs, butter, and ¼ cup sugar and pat onto the bottom of a 9- by 3-inch springform pan. Pour the cheese mixture into the pan. Bake for 45 minutes, or until the top cracks. Cool for 30 minutes.

Mix the sour cream with the remaining 2 tablespoons of sugar. Spread the mixture over the top of the cheesecake and sprinkle with the

17

Willard and Victor Mayeron, owner of The Mucky Duck, after eating their fill of Key Lime Pie. (Photo courtesy of Victor W. Mayeron)

blanched almonds. Bake at 350 degrees for 5 minutes more. The cake *should set for 24 hours.* Serve topped with your favorite fruits, if desired. *Makes 8 to 12 servings.*

★

There are at least three reasons that I'm rather partial to The Mucky Duck Restaurant down in Captiva Island, Florida, right on the Gulf Coast.

First of all, I own property on Captiva Island, and The Mucky Duck has become one of my main kitchens-away-from-home.

Second, I get a great kick out of listening to my friend Victor Mayeron, the owner who styles himself the "Head Duck." He even does his own rendition of Florida bird calls throughout dinner!

Finally, and most important of all, there's the incredible food, like this fantastic Key Lime Pie.

☆   Mucky Duck Homemade Key Lime Pie   ☆

1 8-ounce can sweetened
   condensed milk
7 tablespoons bottled lime juice
3 large egg whites

1 prepared 9-inch graham
   cracker pie shell
Whipped cream for garnish

Mix the sweetened condensed milk with the lime juice in a large mixing bowl.

In another bowl, whip the egg whites until you find you can almost turn the bowl over without them falling out.

Add the egg whites to the bowl with the condensed milk and lime juice. Mix slowly with a whisk so as not to deflate the whipped whites. Pour the mixture into the pie shell and freeze. Serve sliced and topped with whipped cream.
Makes 6 to 8 servings.

★

Whenever I think of The Pirates' House Restaurant down in Savannah, Georgia, I always associate it with a great little Corvair that I bought in the early 1960s. I had done a local TV show in the Washington–Baltimore area, and some merchants in the area introduced this white Corvair convertible on the show. It was the first one that the public had ever seen, and I fell in love with it instantly. In fact, I asked them if I could buy it on the spot, but they said, "No, we can't sell it— it's the only one we've got right now!"

But I kept after them, and finally they sold it to me.

About two weeks later, my wife Mary and I drove the Corvair to Florida, and on the way down we stopped in Savannah for a meal. It was Sunday, and we knew the only place to go for a great Sunday meal was The Pirates' House, which was open from 11:30 A.M. until late in the evening.

As it happened, one of the biggest hits at The Pirates' House that day was our little white Corvair, because nobody, but *nobody,* had ever seen one before. By then my fascination with the Corvair had passed, but I was happy that the other customers were occupied. While they were hanging around the car in the parking lot, I was able to slip ahead of them and snare a couple of my favorite desserts at The Pirates' House, including the restaurant's famous Black Bottom Pie and an incredible Peanut Butter Cream Pie!

☆ Black Bottom Pie ☆

CRUST
½ package Nabisco Famous
  Chocolate Wafers, crushed
¼ cup (½ stick) butter or
  margarine, melted

FILLING
1 envelope unflavored gelatin
¼ cup cold water
4 cups milk
5 eggs, separated

1 cup sugar
½ cup all-purpose flour
2 1-ounce squares unsweetened
  chocolate
1 teaspoon vanilla extract
½ cup dark rum
¼ teaspoon cream of tartar
Whipped cream, miniature
  chocolate chips, and a cherry
  for garnish

To make the crust, preheat the oven to 350 degrees. Combine the cookie crumbs and butter. (This can be done in a food processor.) Press onto the bottom and sides of a 9-inch pie pan. Bake for 7 to 8 minutes, or until set. Cool.

To make filling, dissolve the gelatin in cold water and set aside to soften.

Bring the milk to a rolling boil in a heavy saucepan. Be careful that it doesn't boil over. Meanwhile, beat the egg yolks and ¾ cup of sugar with a wire whisk until thick. Beat in the flour until smooth. When the milk boils, pour it slowly and carefully into the egg mixture, whisking constantly. Whisk until smooth. Pour the mixture back into the milk pan and return to the heat. Bring to a boil over medium heat, whisking constantly. Lower the heat and cook for 2 to 3 minutes, stirring constantly to prevent scorching.

Place the chocolate in a bowl. Pour 2½ cups of the hot custard over the chocolate. Immediately place a piece of plastic wrap directly on the surface of the custard to prevent a skin from forming. If you fail to do this, you will have lumps in your pie.

Let the whole thing sit until the chocolate has melted; then add the vanilla, and stir to blend. Next, replace the plastic wrap. Cool to room temperature and fill the pie crust, spreading the chocolate custard to the edge of the crust. Refrigerate.

Add the gelatin to the remaining hot custard and stir until the gelatin melts. Cover with a plastic wrap, as you did with the chocolate custard. Cool. Stir in the rum. Refrigerate, stirring occasionally, until the custard begins to thicken to about the consistency of unbeaten egg whites.

Beat egg whites and the cream of tartar until they form soft peaks. Then, beat in the remaining ¼ cup of sugar; continue beating until the peaks are stiff but not dry.

Fold the thickened rum custard into the egg whites and mound the top of the chocolate custard in the pie shell. If the rum mixture does not set up, which is highly possible in a hot kitchen, refrigerate it, stirring frequently with a rubber spatula, until it thickens enough to mound. Refrigerate, uncovered, for 4 to 6 hours, or overnight. Garnish with whipped cream, tiny chocolate chips, and a cherry!
Makes 8 servings.

☆ The Peanut Butter Cream Pie ☆

¼ cup creamy peanut butter
½ cup confectioner's sugar
1 baked and cooled 9-inch pie crust
1 cup plus 4 tablespoons granulated sugar
4 tablespoons cornstarch
¼ teaspoon salt

1 13-ounce can evaporated milk
4 large egg yolks, beaten
1½ cups hot water
¼ cup (½ stick) butter, softened
1 teaspoon vanilla extract
4 large egg whites
¼ teaspoon cream of tartar

Preheat the oven to 350 degrees. Rub peanut butter and confectioner's sugar between your fingers until they're crumbly and well combined. Spread in bottom of pie shell. Mix together 1 cup of the sugar, cornstarch, and salt in a heavy saucepan. Whisk in the evaporated milk and egg yolks.

Place over medium heat and slowly whisk in the hot water. Cook, whisking constantly, until the mixture comes to a boil and thickens enough to stand a spoon in. Remove from the heat and stir in the butter and vanilla; then beat until smooth. Pour the custard over the peanut butter mixture in the pie shell.

Beat the egg whites and cream of tartar until soft peaks form. Then beat in the remaining sugar 1 tablespoon at a time and continue beating until stiff but not dry. Spread the meringue over custard filling, making sure to bring all the way out to the crust. Bake for 10 to 15 minutes, or until the meringue has browned.
Makes 8 servings.

★

One of my favorite eating spots near my home in Virginia is the Wayside Inn which unfortunately recently suffered a serious fire. But I understand that plans are already under way to rebuild it, and when the place is back in business you can bet that this "fearsome foursome" of desserts will be available: Ambrosia Pie, Deep-Dish Apple Pie, Wayside Inn's Pecan Pie, and Wayside Inn's Carrot Cake.

☆ Ambrosia Pie ☆

⅔ cup granulated sugar
¼ cup cornstarch
½ teaspoon salt
3 cups milk
4 large egg yolks, well beaten
2 tablespoons butter, softened
1 tablespoon plus 1 teaspoon
  vanilla extract

1 cup flaked coconut
1 baked 9-inch pie shell
1 cup heavy cream
¼ cup confectioner's sugar
¼ cup flaked coconut, toasted
Mandarin orange sections

Combine the granulated sugar, cornstarch, and salt in a large saucepan; mix well. In a bowl, combine the milk and egg yolks and mix well; stir into the sugar mixture. Cook over medium heat, stirring constantly, until the mixture thickens and boils; then boil 1 minute, stirring constantly. Remove from the heat and add the butter, vanilla, and 1 cup of coconut. Let the entire mixture cool; then spoon it into the pie shell.

Whip the cream until it is slightly thickened; add the confectioner's sugar and beat until light and fluffy. Spread over the pie filling, sprinkle with toasted coconut, and garnish with mandarin orange sections. *Makes 10 to 12 servings.*

☆ Deep-Dish Apple Pie ☆

1 pound pie dough or one frozen
  pie shell
1¼ to 1½ cups sugar
⅛ teaspoon salt
¾ teaspoon ground cinnamon
½ teaspoon ground nutmeg
3 tablespoons flour

2 pounds tart apples, peeled,
  cored, and sliced
½ teaspoon grated lemon rind
1 tablespoon fresh lemon juice
  (optional)
1 to 2 tablespoons butter

Preheat the oven to 350 degrees. Line a pie pan with two thirds of the dough. Cover the remaining dough with plastic wrap to keep it moist.

In a large bowl, mix together the sugar, salt, cinnamon, nutmeg, and flour. Add the sliced apples and mix well so the apples are coated with the other ingredients. Place the apple slices in the pie pan, laying slices first along the outside and then working toward the center until the bottom of the pastry shell is covered.

Continue layering the slices in the same way until the shell is completely filled. Sprinkle the apples with the lemon rind and juice and dot with the butter. Moisten the edge of the shell. Roll out the remaining dough and cover the pie with the dough. Trim the edge of the dough to a ½-inch overhang. Press the edges firmly together, flute, and then slash vents in the center of the top of the pie. Bake for 30 to 40 minutes, or until the apples are tender and the crust is golden brown.
Makes 10 to 12 servings.

☆ Wayside Inn's Pecan Pie ☆

PASTRY
⅔ cup vegetable shortening
2 cups all-purpose flour
½ teaspoon salt
4 to 5 tablespoons ice water

FILLING
3 large eggs

⅔ cup packed dark brown sugar
½ teaspoon salt
⅓ cup butter, melted
1 cup dark or light corn syrup
1 cup pecan halves or broken
   pecans

To make the pastry, cut shortening into flour and salt with pastry blender. As soon as the shortening is well coated with flour, rub with your fingertips until the mixture looks like fine crumbs. Then make a well in the center and pour in 4 tablespoons of the ice water. Mix quickly with a knife and add more water if necessary to give a firm, not sticky, dough. Preheat the oven to 375 degrees.

To make the filling, combine the eggs, sugar, salt, butter, and syrup in a bowl. Beat with a rotary beater. Cover the bottom of the pie shell with the pecans. Pour the filling over the nuts. Bake for 40 to 50 minutes, or until the filling is set.
Makes 6 to 8 servings.

☆ Wayside Inn's Carrot Cake ☆

CAKE
2 cups sugar
4 eggs
1½ cups oil
2 cups self-rising flour
1½ teaspoons baking soda
2 teaspoons cinnamon
2 cups grated carrots
Nuts (optional)

ICING
½ cup (1 stick) butter
1 1-pound box confectioner's
  sugar
1 teaspoon vanilla extract
1 8-ounce package cream cheese
Nuts and flaked coconut
  (optional)

To make the cake, preheat the oven to 350 degrees. Slowly beat sugar, eggs, and oil together very well. Add flour, baking soda, and cinnamon; mix well. Fold in carrots. Add nuts if desired (black walnuts are good); mix until well blended. Bake for 40 minutes in a 9- by 13- by 2-inch sheet cake pan.

To make the icing, mix all ingredients together and spread on cake when cool.
Makes 10 to 12 servings.

★

The Sea Captain's House in Myrtle Beach, South Carolina, is so close to the water that you think you can reach over and splash around in it. There are actually three restaurant locations under the same ownership in the area, but the one I particularly like is built like a little beach cottage.

They took me through the kitchen there, and if I've ever seen a group of workers who seemed the picture of happiness and contentment, it was the cooking and kitchen staff at that little restaurant. Also, the place was really spotless. You could have eaten off the floor in any corner in that kitchen. While I was visiting there, one of the desserts they were preparing was a fantastic cheesecake, which has a rather unusual history.

It seems that after the owners of Sea Captain's House had looked high and low for the perfect cheesecake recipe a number of years ago, they were finally directed to a woman from Charlotte, North Carolina.

She had married a gentleman from New York City who was extremely fond of cheesecake, but only the way his mother made it. To bolster her husband's opinion of her, the woman resolved to prepare a cheesecake which would be comparable to that of her mother-in-law. But each time she tried, her husband would shake his head and say, "Good, but not like my mother's!"

After failing for many years to reach her goal, this woman began to suffer increasing self-doubts about her ability to consummate the culinary side of her marriage. But then, just when she thought she might never be able to measure up, she finally produced a cheesecake which made her husband exclaim, "Just as good as Mom's!"

Soon afterward, she passed the recipe on to the Sea Captain's House, which dubbed the dish . . .

☆ The Save-a-Marriage Cheesecake ☆

GRAHAM-NUT CRUST
1¾ cups fine graham cracker
   crumbs
¼ cup pecans, chopped fine
½ teaspoon ground cinnamon
¼ cup (½ stick) butter, melted

FILLING
3 large eggs, beaten

2 8-ounce packages cream
   cheese, softened
2 teaspoons vanilla extract
½ teaspoon almond extract
1 cup sugar
¼ teaspoon salt
3 cups sour cream

To make the crust, mix together all the crust ingredients. Press the mixture onto the sides and bottom of a buttered 9-inch springform pan. Reserve a little of mixture to trim the cake.

To make the filling, preheat oven to 375 degrees. Combine all ingredients *except* the sour cream. Beat until smooth. Blend in the sour cream and pour into the prepared graham-nut crust. Trim with reserve crumbs. Bake for 35 minutes, or until set.
Makes 10 to 14 servings.

★

The Bubble Room on Captiva Island in Florida is a place that I fell in love with the first time I walked through the doors.

The whole place is permeated with nostalgia. When you first drive onto the grounds, you pass an old-fashioned fire engine, where your kids can climb and play to their hearts' content.

The nostalgia theme continues when you enter the restaurant. The first thing that strikes you is the music they play all the time—pieces from the thirties, forties, and fifties. You might hear Doris Day singing "Que Sera, Sera," Bing Crosby crooning "White Christmas," or maybe Vaughan Monroe belting out "Ghost Riders in the Sky."

Memorabilia from the thirties and forties lines the walls, including pictures of many old movie stars and early TV performers. You'll also see an extensive collection of the famous bubble Christmas lights from the 1950s, the ones with the liquid that bubbles up in lighted glass containers. Of course, that's where the restaurant got its name.

When I order a meal at this restaurant, I never hold back. In fact, the owners of the Bubble Room, Katie and Jamie Farquharson, made me a charter member of their "Bubble Room Big Boys Club," because I actually finished their two-and-a-half-pound prime rib!

And I don't stop with the beef! Every time I've been in there, I've always managed to leave plenty of room for their super desserts. The desserts there are among my favorites anywhere in the country, and here are a couple that have particularly struck my fancy.

The Red Velvet cake is a quick-to-make crowd-pleaser.

☆ Red Velvet Cake ☆

CAKE
2½ cups self-rising flour
1 cup buttermilk
1½ cups vegetable oil
1 teaspoon baking soda
1 teaspoon vanilla extract
¼ cup red food coloring
1½ cups sugar
1 teaspoon unsweetened cocoa
  powder
1 teaspoon white vinegar
2 large eggs

FROSTING
⅓ pound (1⅓ sticks) butter,
  softened
1 1-pound box confectioner's
  sugar
10 ounces cream cheese,
  softened
1½ cups chopped pecans

To make the cake, preheat oven to 350 degrees. Mix together all ingredients with an electric mixer. Spray three 9-inch-round cake pans with nonstick coating. Pour the batter equally into the three pans and bake for 5 minutes. Test for doneness with a toothpick.

To make the frosting, combine the butter, cream cheese, and sugar in a bowl. Beat until fluffy; then fold in the pecans. Use to frost the cake when it is cool.
Makes 10 to 15 servings.

This next dessert will knock your socks off.

☆ Chocolate Cappuccino Mint Cheesecake ☆

FILLING
1 6-ounce package semisweet
   chocolate bits
1 teaspoon instant cappuccino
   coffee crystals
2 8-ounce packages cream
   cheese, softened
½ cup sour cream
⅓ cup sugar
¼ cup lemon juice
¾ tablespoons vanilla extract
3 large eggs at room
   temperature

CRUST
2½ cups graham cracker crumbs
¼ cup sugar
18 fresh mint leaves or ½
   teaspoon mint extract
¼ cup (½ stick) butter, melted

GARNISH
½ cup sour cream
12 fresh strawberries, sliced
Shaved semisweet chocolate

To make the filling, preheat the oven to 350 degrees. Melt the chocolate in the top of a double boiler with the coffee crystals over just simmering water.

Cut the cream cheese at room temperature; then slice it into pieces, and put it into a mixing bowl. Beat it on slow speed and add sour cream. Blend until smooth. Add sugar, lemon juice, and vanilla. Beat in the eggs one at a time. Very slowly, add chocolate, and beat for 2 minutes.

To make the crust, mix graham cracker crumbs and sugar together. (If using mint extract, mix the extract into the graham cracker crumbs.) Blend in the butter with a wooden spoon. Lightly brush the bottom of a 10-inch springform pan with butter and, if using fresh mint leaves, place them on the bottom of the pan. Pour the graham cracker mixture on top. With a wooden spoon, press the mixture down until an even crust is formed.

(Continued)

Pour the cheese mixture on top of the crust and bake for 55 minutes. Then turn the oven off and use a wooden spoon to hold the oven door open. Let the cheesecake cool for 1 hour in the oven.

Release the sides of the springform and, using a pastry frosting knife inserted under the crust, carefully lift the cake off the springform pan bottom. Peel mint leaves away and place cheesecake on a doily.

To garnish, spread the sour cream all over the top of the cake. Add sliced fresh strawberries and shaved chocolate.
Makes 10 to 14 servings.

★

In my humble opinion, the Regency Dining Room at the Williamsburg Inn in Colonial Williamsburg is one of the most elegant dining rooms in the entire United States. The service is superb and the waiters and waitresses are gracious and elegant: They even have someone strumming on a harp to provide background music for your dinner!

So if you really want to "go elegant" at home with your sweet tooth, try these two desserts from the Regency Dining Room.

☆ Regency Hazelnut-Ice Cream Cake ☆

1¾ cups hazelnuts
4 large egg yolks
2 cups granulated sugar
½ teaspoon salt
¼ cup all-purpose flour
8 cups light cream, scalded
2½ teaspoons vanilla extract
½ teaspoon almond extract

1 10-inch spongecake (made
   from a mix)
Hazelnut Meringue (recipe
   follows)
1 cup heavy cream
2 tablespoons confectioner's
   sugar

Preheat the oven to 350 degrees.

Put the hazelnuts on a baking sheet and bake for 15 to 20 minutes. Cover and let stand for 10 minutes. Rub the nuts between the palms of your hands or in a towel to remove the thin skins. Then grind the nuts to a fine powder in a food processor or blender. Set them aside.

Beat the egg yolks, sugar, salt, and flour until well blended. Gradually pour the scalded cream over the egg mixture, beating constantly. Cook over medium heat, stirring constantly, until the mixture thickens. Do not let the mixture boil. Remove from the heat. Add 2 teaspoons of the vanilla and the almond extract. Fold in the hazelnuts. Cover and chill thoroughly.

Pour the mixture into the freezer container of an electric ice-cream maker and freeze following the manufacturer's instructions.

Remove the ice cream from the freezer and let it soften for 10 minutes before spreading it on the cake.

Freeze the spongecake for 10 minutes. Slice the spongecake in half, horizontally. Place half on a cake plate and reserve the other half for another use.

Spread the softened ice cream on top of the cake. The ice cream should be about 2½ inches thick. The sides should be straight and the top as flat as possible.

Place the Hazelnut Meringue on top of the ice cream. Return to the freezer.

Whip the cream until stiff. Then whip in the remaining ½ teaspoon of vanilla and the confectioner's sugar.

Frost the top and sides of the cake with three quarters of the whipped cream.

Place the remaining whipped cream in a pastry bag fitted with a decorative tip. Make rosettes of whipped cream around the top of the cake. Now, you're ready to serve!

Makes 8 to 12 servings.

☆ Hazelnut Meringue ☆

1 large egg white	¼ cup sugar
pinch of salt	2 tablespoons ground hazelnuts

Preheat the oven to 250 degrees. Trace a 10-inch circle on a piece of parchment paper. Place the paper on a baking sheet.

Beat the egg white until frothy. Add the salt and beat until soft peaks form. Gradually add the sugar, beating until stiff peaks form. Fold in the hazelnuts.

Place the meringue in the center of the parchment circle. Smooth it evenly to the outer edge with a small spatula.

Bake for 30 minutes. Turn off the oven, leaving the meringue in the oven for 1 hour. Turn on the oven again to 250 degrees and bake for an additional 30 minutes. Turn off the oven. Let the meringue remain in the oven without opening the door for at least 2 hours.

★

Of course, not every good dish in this country comes from a restaurant, not by any means!

For example, you might want to try a couple of great, traditional cake recipes passed on to me by Adina Taylor, an architect who was born in Canada, reared in Florida, and who presently lives in New York.

Adina travels extensively, so she gets plenty of opportunity to sample the food all over this country and in other parts of the world. But she still comes back to these two dessert recipes, which have been handed down from generation to generation in her family.

☆ Adina Taylor's Birthday Cake ☆

2 cups all-purpose flour	½ teaspoon salt
1¼ cups sugar	1 teaspoon lemon juice
2 teaspoons baking powder	1 teaspoon vanilla extract
½ cup (1 stick) butter	1 teaspoon almond extract
⅔ cup milk	3 large eggs

Preheat the oven to 300 degrees. Grease 9″ angel food cake pan and dust with flour. Mix together flour, sugar, baking powder, butter, milk, salt, lemon, vanilla, and almond extract. Then add 3 eggs, one at a time.

Bake 45 minutes. Ice the cake with your favorite frosting.
Makes 8 to 12 servings.

☆ Adina Taylor Chiffon Layer Cake ☆

The meringue is the key to this cake, by the way, so give it your special attention! To get the best results, Adina suggests we follow the directions exactly.

2 large eggs, separated	⅓ cup vegetable oil
1½ cups sugar	1 cup buttermilk
1¾ cups all-purpose flour	2 1-ounce squares unsweetened
¾ teaspoon baking soda	chocolate, melted
¾ teaspoon salt	

Preheat the oven to 350 degrees. Grease 2 layer pans and dust them with flour.

To make the meringue, beat the egg whites until they're frothy. Then gradually beat ½ cup of the sugar into the egg whites. Continue beating until the mixture is stiff and glossy.

To make the batter, sift the remaining sugar, flour, baking soda, and salt into another bowl. Add the oil and ½ cup of the buttermilk into this mixture. Beat the mixture for 1 minute and add the remaining buttermilk, egg yolks, and chocolate.

Fold the meringue into the batter by cutting down gently through the batter across the bottom of the bowl, moving up and over and turning the bowl as you go. After you've finished the folding, pour the batter into the prepared pans. Bake for 30 to 35 minutes. Ice the cake with your favorite frosting.

Makes 8 to 12 servings.

Note: Whole milk may be substituted for the buttermilk.

Finally, here's some further evidence that Adina's family tradition is "squared away" in the dessert department!

☆ Raspberry Squares ☆

BATTER	TOPPING
1 large egg	1 large egg
1 cup sifted all-purpose flour	1 cup sugar
1 teaspoon baking powder	¼ cup (½ stick) butter, melted
½ cup (1 stick) butter, softened	2 cups flaked coconut
1 tablespoon milk	1 teaspoon vanilla extract
1 10-ounce jar raspberry jam	

Preheat the oven to 350 degrees. To make the batter, beat the egg and set it aside. Then sift the flour and baking powder together into a bowl. Work the butter into the flour with your fingertips until the mixture is mealy. Stir in the beaten egg and milk. Mix well. Spread the batter mixture in bottom of 8-inch-square pan. Cover the batter with a layer of jam to taste. Now, you're ready to gather together the ingredients for the delicious topping.

To make the topping, beat the egg in a bowl. Stir the sugar into the egg; then mix in the melted butter, coconut, and vanilla. Spread the

mixture on top of the jam. Bake for about 30 minutes, or until the topping is brown.
Makes 16 servings.

☆ Granny's Fruit Squares ☆

1¼ cups all-purpose flour	½ cup chopped walnuts
1 tablespoon confectioner's sugar	1 teaspoon vanilla extract
	1 cup packed brown sugar
½ cup (1 stick) butter, softened	1 teaspoon baking powder
½ teaspoon salt	1 cup chopped pitted dates
2 large eggs, beaten	¼ cup flaked coconut

Preheat the oven to 350 degrees. Sift together 1 cup of the flour and the confectioner's sugar in a bowl. Then mix in the butter and ¼ teaspoon of the salt. Press the mixture into an 8-inch-square pan. Bake for 10 minutes.

In a bowl, mix together the eggs, remaining flour, remaining salt, walnuts, vanilla, brown sugar, baking powder, dates, and coconut. Spread this second mixture on top of the first and bake for 20 minutes. Cool on a wire rack and cut into squares to serve.
Makes 10 to 16 servings.

★

If you want to discover the heart of Yankee America, the Down-East Village Restaurant in Yarmouth, Maine, is the place to go.

One big advantage of the Down-East Village Restaurant is that it's located quite near the famous L. L. Bean Store. As far as I'm concerned, a pilgrimage to L. L. Bean is a pilgrimage to America, like going to the Grand Canyon or Mt. Rushmore.

Anybody who goes into L. L. Bean and stays there for just an hour might as well have stayed away. You've got to stay there at least two days if you're going to really check out all their clothes and outdoor products. And if you *do* stay in the area for a couple of days, the only place to sleep and eat is the Down-East Village Restaurant and Motel.

For starters, try this Blueberry Cobbler, which Innkeepers Ed and Sue Ferrell offer as a specialty of the house. Later, I'll include some of their other specialties, such as blueberry muffins and pancakes.

☆ Blueberry Cobbler ☆

FILLING
2 cups blueberries, stemmed,
    washed, and drained
¼ cup all-purpose flour
1 teaspoon ground cinnamon

½ teaspoon salt
½ cup sugar
1 large egg, beaten
¾ cup milk
½ cup (1 stick) butter, melted

TOPPING
1½ cups all-purpose flour
2 teaspoons baking powder

Preheat the oven to 425 degrees. In a bowl, mix together the blueberries, flour, and cinnamon. Pour the mixture into a buttered 8-inch-square pan.

In a bowl, mix together all the topping ingredients. Cover the blueberry mixture in the pan with topping. Bake for 35 to 40 minutes. Serve hot topped with vanilla ice cream.
Makes 10 to 16 servings.

★

As you know, I like to cook, too. The great British actor Robert Morley apparently found out somewhere about my avocation and asked me to appear with him on his program, which is aired on the CBN Cable Network.

Although I'm not by any means a gourmet cook, I do have a rather exotic taste in sweets. So I cooked what's been called Willard Scott's Rain or Shine Chestnut Cloud Pudding—an appropriate dish for a weatherman, wouldn't you say?!

When two Celebrity Chefs—actor Robert Morley and Willard—joined culinary forces, the results were "heavenly." (Photo courtesy of Celebrity Chefs © 1985 Mary Bloom/Creative Programming Inc.)

☆ Rain or Shine Chestnut Cloud Pudding ☆

PUDDING
2½ cups (1 15½-ounce can) drained unsweetened whole chestnuts
1 cup sugar
4 large eggs, separated
⅔ cup butter, softened
¼ cup heavy cream
3 tablespoons dark rum
1 tablespoon vanilla extract

¼ cup all-purpose flour
2 1-ounce squares unsweetened chocolate, melted and cooled

TOPPING
1½ cups cold heavy cream
2 tablespoons sugar
½ teaspoon vanilla extract
Candied violets

To prepare the pudding, preheat the oven to 350 degrees. In a food processor or blender, purée the chestnuts with the sugar. Add the egg yolks and process until well combined. Add the butter, heavy cream, rum, vanilla, and flour. Process until well combined.

In a small mixing bowl, beat the egg whites until stiff but not dry. Fold into the chestnut mixture. Pour half of the batter into a second mixing bowl; stir in the melted chocolate. With three stirs, swirl the plain chestnut mixture into the chocolate mixture.

Carefully pour the batter into a well-greased round, 6-cup ovenproof bowl or mold, disturbing the swirls as little as possible.

Place the bowl in a pan filled with hot water to approximately the same level as the pudding surface. Bake for 1½ hours, or until the top of the pudding is firm and the center does not wiggle when the bowl is shaken gently. Remove from the water and cool completely on a wire rack.

Loosen the sides of the pudding carefully with a flexible metal spatula. Turn the pudding out onto a serving plate. Cover and refrigerate for 4 hours or overnight.

To prepare the topping, whip 1½ cups of the cream with the sugar and vanilla until stiff peaks form. Spoon into a pastry bag fitted with a small star tip. Pipe the cream onto the pudding, covering it completely. Garnish with candied violets. Cut into wedges to serve.
Makes 8 servings.

★

Austrians have a special knack for putting together wonderful desserts, and when they begin to tailor their dishes to the American scene, they get even better.

One of my favorite Austrian restaurants in New York City is Vienna '79, and here are some examples of their top desserts, which they've so kindly shared with me.

☆ Raspberry Flambé ☆

In this dish, the tangy flavor of raspberries and the sparkling "essence of oranges" harmonize in a way that captures the joy of an Austrian summer. This adds a tantalizing and airy conclusion to an elegant dinner.

¾ cup orange juice	2 tablespoons cornstarch
2 tablespoons granulated sugar	¾ cup heavy cream
⅓ cup Grand Marnier plus a bit to flambé	2 pints fresh raspberries, rinsed and drained
4 large egg yolks	

Preheat the oven to 500 degrees. Combine the orange juice and sugar in a saucepan, bring to a boil, and reduce by half. Allow to cool a bit.

(*Continued*)

Meanwhile, combine the Grand Marnier, egg yolks, and cornstarch in a bowl. Whisk until smooth. Slowly stir the Grand Marnier mixture into the orange juice. Bring just to the boiling point, stirring constantly. Set aside and allow to cool.

Whip the cream and fold it into the custard.

Distribute the raspberries in six individual baking dishes. Cover the berries with the Grand Marnier mixture and bake approximately 20 minutes until golden brown. Remove from the oven, and pour a few drops of Grand Marnier over each dish and ignite, using a long kitchen match. Serve immediately.

Makes 6 servings.

☆ Salzburger Nockerln ☆

Golden peaks and gossamer cloudlets of meringue make this specialty, which is named for Mozart's birthplace, an irresistible dessert soufflé. The folks at Vienna '79 call it their "ethereal delight," and it should be served right from the oven.

4 teaspoons currant or grape
   jelly
4 tablespoons whipped cream
4 teaspoons unsalted butter
   (never use salted butter in
   Vienna '79 recipes)
9 large egg whites

½ cup vanilla sugar (Put 1 or 2
   split vanilla beans in a sealed
   canister of sugar for 48
   hours.)
Juice of ½ lemon
4 egg yolks
½ cup sifted all-purpose flour

Preheat the oven to 450 degrees. Place 4 1-cup soufflé dishes on a baking sheet. In each dish, place 1 teaspoon of jelly, 1 tablespoon of whipped cream, and 1 teaspoon of butter.

Combine the egg whites, vanilla sugar, and lemon juice in a metal bowl. Beat with an electric mixer at high speed until stiff peaks are formed. Gently fold the egg yolks and flour into the meringue. Use a spatula to place 3 large mounds of the mixture into each baking dish. Smooth the surface of each and bake for 8 minutes, or until puffed and golden. Serve immediately.

Makes 4 servings.

☆ Topfenknodel (Farmer Cheese Dumplings) ☆

A breeze to make, these plump dumplings, fragrant with vanilla, are luscious by themselves and really a knockout when served with plum sauce.

¾ cup (1½ sticks) butter
1 tablespoon vanilla sugar (Put 1 or 2 split vanilla beans in a sealed canister of sugar for 48 hours.)
2 large eggs
Grated rind of ½ lemon
Juice of ½ lemon

10½ ounces farmer cheese, pressed through a sieve
¼ cup semolina
Pinch of salt
Scant ½ cup dry bread crumbs
3 tablespoons confectioner's sugar
Plum Sauce (recipe follows)

Combine 2 tablespoons of the butter, vanilla sugar, eggs, lemon rind, and lemon juice in a bowl. Beat until frothy. Add the strained farmer cheese and beat until smooth. Beat in the semolina and refrigerate for an hour.

Bring a pot of water with a pinch of salt to a boil. With an ice-cream scooper, form 12 round dumplings. Drop the dumplings into the water and simmer for approximately 15 minutes. The dumplings will rise to the surface when done.

In a frying pan, melt the remaining butter and brown the bread crumbs. Remove the dumplings with a slotted spoon and drain them. Roll the dumplings in the bread crumbs.

Serve 2 warm dumplings per person, sprinkling them with confectioner's sugar. The Topfenknodel may be served with plum sauce.
Makes 6 servings.

☆ Plum Sauce ☆

½ to 1 cup water
Juice of 1 lemon
⅞ cup crystallized or granulated sugar

1 cinnamon stick
2 to 4 whole cloves
2 pounds ripe plums with pits removed

37

Bring the water, lemon juice, sugar, cinnamon, and cloves to a boil. Add the plums and simmer, stirring constantly, until the skins are shriveled.

Remove the plums with a slotted spoon. Reduce the remaining liquid by half, strain and pour over the fruit. Allow to cool, cover, and refrigerate.

☆ Farmer Cheese Soufflé with Strawberry Sauce ☆

I'm on the same wavelength with those Austrians who love farmer cheese desserts. Accompanied by a fresh strawberry sauce, this is an exciting dish, perfect for concluding any dinner on a tasty note.

4 large eggs, separated
Scant ¼ cup granulated sugar
Grated rind of 1 lemon
3½ ounces farmer cheese
¼ cup confectioner's sugar
Juice of 1 lemon

Butter and 1 tablespoon confectioner's sugar, for spreading in the individual soufflé molds
1 pint fresh strawberries, stems removed

Preheat the oven to 400 degrees. Combine the egg yolks, granulated sugar, and lemon rind in a bowl, and whip until creamy. Strain the farmer cheese through a fine sieve into the egg yolks and whip until smooth. In a separate bowl, beat the egg whites, confectioner's sugar, and lemon juice to a stiff meringue. Carefully fold the meringue into the farmer cheese mixture.

Butter 6 individual soufflé dishes and sprinkle them with confectioner's sugar. Pour in the mixture, leaving ¼ inch of room at the top to allow for expansion. Place the soufflé dishes in a roasting pan. Fill the pan with hot water to come halfway up the sides of the molds. Bake for 35 minutes.

Meanwhile, purée the strawberries in a food processor; then strain and sweeten to taste.

Remove the molds from the oven and place them on individual dessert plates. Serve the strawberry sauce separately. You may also unmold the soufflés on individual plates and surround them with the sauce.
Makes 6 servings.

☆ Warm Chocolate Almond Cake ☆

You can really pamper your guests with this rich, flourless confection, served right from the oven in individual molds.

4 ounces sweet dark chocolate
½ cup (1 stick) butter, softened
½ cup sugar
9 large eggs, separated

4 ounces blanched almonds, ground
Scant ½ cup dry bread crumbs
Whipped cream
Chocolate Sauce (recipe follows)

Preheat the oven to 350 degrees. Melt the chocolate in a bowl over steaming water. Allow to cool.

With an electric mixer, cream the butter and sugar together in a large bowl. Add the egg yolks and blend well. Beat in the chocolate and then the ground almonds and bread crumbs.

In a separate bowl, whisk the egg whites until stiff and carefully fold them into the batter.

Butter 16 tall individual baking dishes and pour in the batter. Place the dishes in a roasting pan with hot water that comes halfway up the sides of the dishes. Bake for 25 minutes, cover the pan with aluminum foil, and bake 10 minutes more.

Serve warm with whipped cream and the following chocolate sauce. *Makes 16 servings.*

☆ Chocolate Sauce ☆

11½ ounces sweet dark chocolate

5 tablespoons sugar
½ cup heavy cream

Melt the chocolate in a bowl over steaming water. Stir in the sugar.

Pour the heavy cream into a saucepan and add the melted chocolate mixture. Bring quickly to a boil and remove from the heat immediately.

★

I first discovered the Stock Yard Inn in Lancaster, Pennsylvania, when I was in the Navy. I had been in boot camp in Maryland, and the first week that I was out on leave, I headed straight up to Pennsylvania Dutch Country with a buddy of mine.

The first place we stopped was Lancaster, and the first restaurant we headed for was the Stock Yard Inn. The historic building was constructed between 1750 and 1775 as an old homestead. It remained a homestead until 1900, when it was converted into a restaurant. In the pre-restaurant period, however, the place was owned for a while by President James Buchanan. (He was the proprietor from 1856 to 1864.) President Buchanan was on to a good thing. I'll never forget that meal, even though it was back in 1955, more than thirty years ago. I had a steak and a great dessert, and ever since I've had a warm spot in my heart for the Stock Yard Inn.

Since those boot camp days, I've returned to Lancaster and the Stock Yard Inn several times, and I can honestly say that the quality of the food there has always remained consistently delicious. If you don't believe me, try this Chocolate Mousse Pie from their kitchen.

☆ Chocolate Mousse Pie ☆

FILLING
1 pound semisweet chocolate
2 large eggs
3 large egg yolks
4 large egg whites at room
   temperature
6 tablespoons confectioner's
   sugar

4 cups heavy cream
Granulated sugar to taste

CRUST
3 cups Nabisco Famous
   Chocolate Wafer crumbs
¼ pound sweet butter

To make the crust, combine crumbs and butter. Press onto the bottom and completely up the sides of a 10-inch springform pan. Refrigerate for 30 minutes.

To make the filling, soften the chocolate in the top of a double boiler over simmering water. Let cool to 95 degrees on a candy thermometer. Add the whole eggs and mix well. Add the egg yolks and mix until thoroughly blended.

Whip 2 cups of the cream with the confectioner's sugar until soft peaks form. Beat egg whites until they're stiff, but not dry. Stir a little of the cream and egg whites into the chocolate mixture to lighten it; then fold in the remaining cream and whites until they are completely incorporated. Turn the filling into the crust, cover, and chill overnight.

When ready to serve, prepare the topping by whipping 2 cups of the cream with granulated sugar to taste until quite stiff.

Loosen the crust of the mousse on all sides, using a sharp knife; remove the sides of the springform pan. Then place the mousse on a serving plate and spread all but about ½ cup of the whipped cream over the top of the mousse. Put the remaining cream into a pastry bag and pipe rosettes in the center of the pie and around the base, if desired. *Makes 10 to 16 servings.*

★

Middleburg, Virginia is grass-roots Willard, and the Coach Stop Restaurant is about as close as you can get to real home cooking in my part of the country.

Restaurants and chefs have come and gone in this part of Virginia, which is the heart of horse country. But the Coach Stop has always remained the local watering hole, with the owners, Brian and Loretta Jillson, serving as the guiding lights for this fine establishment. The Jillsons tell me that their clientele has included former White House aide Michael Deaver, former presidential press secretary James Brady, Senator John Warner, and actors Robert Duvall and Robert Wagner.

But even though the Jillsons are constantly rubbing shoulders with celebrities, they manage to maintain a solid, down-to-earth, family atmosphere. They're so tender-hearted they even let their pet ducks wander around the house and play in a little tub of water in the bathroom. You'll never find roast duck on their menus!

When you finish your meal and are ready for some sweets, be prepared for some home cooking like you never tasted at home! Here are some samples.

☆ Piña Colada Cake ☆

CAKE
1 18.25-ounce box white cake mix
1 3½-ounce box instant vanilla pudding mix
4 large eggs
⅓ cup light rum
¾ cup water
½ cup vegetable oil
1 3½-ounce can flaked coconut

TOPPING
1 3½-ounce box instant vanilla pudding mix
⅓ cup light rum
1 3½-ounce can flaked coconut
1 cup drained crushed pineapple
1 8-ounce container Cool Whip

Preheat the oven to 350 degrees. Generously grease and then flour two 9-inch-round cake pans.

Blend all the ingredients in a large bowl; beat at medium speed for 4 minutes. Bake for 25 to 30 minutes, or until a toothpick inserted in the center comes out clean. Cool completely on a wire rack.

Stir the pudding mix, rum, and coconut, and pineapple together. Blend in Cool Whip and spread on cake.
Makes 12 to 16 servings.

☆ Hunter's Pudding ☆

⅓ cup butter	2 cups bread pieces
1 cup packed light brown sugar	1 cup raisins
1 teaspoon ground cinnamon	½ cup pecan pieces
½ teaspoon ground cloves	⅓ cup dark rum (optional)
½ teaspoon ground nutmeg	1 cup milk
1 large egg	1 teaspoon baking soda

Preheat the oven to 350 degrees. Cream the butter and sugar with the spices; beat in the egg. Add the bread, raisins, nuts, rum, and milk, mixed with baking soda. Pour into a 9-inch-square dish and bake for 1½ hours.
Makes 6 to 8 servings.

★

Many times, the best restaurants you can find are little places sandwiched in here and there in out-of-the-way places.

One of the most delectable little neighborhood restaurants near my place on the Upper East Side in Manhattan is the Bis! Restaurant, which, believe me, you'll be hard-pressed to find if you don't know where to look for it!

The soups are incredible, the entrées are superb, the desserts are divine—and the prices are right.

Quite frankly, I've never tasted rice pudding anywhere that can top what they offer at Bis! For good measure, I've also added a recipe for their Crème Brûlée.

☆ Rich Rice Pudding ☆

1 quart milk	½ cup plus 2 teaspoons sugar
Grated rind of 1 small orange	2 teaspoons vanilla extract
7 tablespoons long-grain rice	⅓ cup heavy cream
Grated rind of 1 lemon	

Combine the milk, orange rind, rice, and lemon rind in a saucepan. Bring to a boil. Then lower the heat to medium and cook for 20 minutes, stirring often. When the pudding starts to thicken and stick to the bottom of the pan (about 20 minutes), lower heat. Cook until quite thick, another 5 to 10 minutes.

Add ½ cup of the sugar and cook for 2 to 3 minutes more. Remove from the heat and cool slightly. Add the vanilla extract. Then cover the mixture and refrigerate for several hours or overnight.

Before serving, thin to the desired consistency with heavy cream. Preheat your broiler. Whip the heavy cream with the remaining sugar and a few drops of vanilla extract until very stiff.

Immediately before serving, divide the pudding into individual heat-proof bowls or a flat 1¼- to 1½-quart heatproof container. In either case, do not fill the dishes higher than within ½ inch of the top.

Divide the whipped cream among the dishes by dropping it in a large dollop in the middle, or placing it in a mound in the middle of the larger dish. Run the pudding under the broiler, with the top of the whipped cream just under the flame. Toast for 2 to 3 minutes, or until the edges of the cream brown; but be careful not to let it burn! Serve immediately. *Makes 4 servings.*

★

The folks at Bis! say, "You can always tell when someone at the restaurant is having our Crème Brûlée. The eyes roll slightly toward heaven, a small moan of pleasure escapes the lips, and the hands move subtly in a protective gesture around the bowl, guarding it against table companions who might want 'just a little taste.' "

Though the ingredients are simple, this dessert requires some care in the making. But the rewards are worth the effort.

☆ Crème Brûlée ☆

2 cups heavy cream	1 teaspoon vanilla extract
6 large egg yolks	2 tablespoons packed dark
6 tablespoons granulated sugar	brown sugar
2 tablespoons Grand Marnier	

Scald heavy cream. Then combine the egg yolks and 4 tablespoons of the sugar in a double boiler. With a wire whisk, beat the yolks constantly over low heat until they begin to thicken. Slowly whisk in the hot cream. Continue to cook and stir over simmering water until the custard is fairly thick—about the consistency of a creamy salad dressing. Do not overcook. If the custard does begin to curdle, remove it from the heat, add a tablespoon of ice water, and beat very hard.

When the custard has thickened, remove it from the heat. Stir in Grand Marnier and vanilla extract. Allow to cool, stirring occasionally. Pour into individual heatproof bowls, cover, and refrigerate for several hours or overnight.

Combine the remaining granulated sugar with the brown sugar and sprinkle over the tops of the custards. The sugar should cover the cream *very* evenly and *very* thinly—about $\frac{1}{16}$ of an inch thick. You may need a little more or a little less sugar, depending on the diameter of your bowls.

Run the bowls under the broiler, close to the flame, for a minute or two, watching carefully until the sugar melts and begins to caramelize.

Return to the refrigerator to cool for at least 10 minutes. When the sugar is cool it will form a hard, glassy covering. To eat, crack the sugar layer with a spoon and discover bliss.
Makes 4 to 6 servings.

Note: The sugar layer will become soft if it is refrigerated for more than a few hours. It may be hardened up again by running *briefly* under the broiler and cooling again, though you run the risk of burning the sugar.

★

One of the great little treasures on Madison Avenue in Manhattan is Woods Restaurant. They've got a fabulous vegetable dish, which we'll salivate over a little later. For now, consider their tasty Chocolate-Mocha Roulade.

☆ Chocolate-Mocha Roulade ☆

CAKE
6 large eggs, separated
2 cups superfine sugar

½ cup unsweetened cocoa powder

FILLING
1 quart (4 cups) heavy cream
2 tablespoons instant espresso coffee powder

2 tablespoons coffee liqueur
2 ounces chocolate, melted, with coffee added to taste

Preheat the oven to 350 degrees. To make the cake, beat the egg yolks in a large bowl on high speed with an electric mixer until thick, about 10 minutes. At low speed, beat in the sugar until completely incorporated; then beat on high speed again for 5 minutes. Sprinkle the cocoa over the egg yolk mixture and beat it in on low speed.

Put the egg whites into a mixing bowl and beat until stiff peaks form. Fold the beaten egg whites into the chocolate batter just until blended. Do not overmix.

Butter a 12- by 18-inch baking pan and line it with parchment paper. Pour the batter into the pan and bake for 40 minutes.

To make the filling, combine all the ingredients in a mixing bowl and beat until stiff.

Turn out the baked roulade onto sugar-sprinkled aluminum foil, and trim the sides of the cake to eliminate the burnt edges.

Brush the top of the cake with melted chocolate (which should have a little bit of coffee added to it). Then spread out the whipped cream evenly and roll the whole thing up by lifting the foil gently and turning one edge into the center.
Makes 15 to 20 servings.

★

Another great New York restaurant is Le Pèrigord Park Restaurant. This place has been around for years, and the atmosphere is reminiscent of a neighborhood café. The staff wears tuxedos, and the food looks as elegant as the waiters do. Still, those waiting on you are friendly, warm, and bubbly; the atmosphere is anything but stuffy, even though the location is a posh Park Avenue address.

☆ Raspberry Mousse ☆

⅝ cup sugar
½ cup water
8 large egg yolks
1 10-ounce jar raspberry jam

2 pounds canned raspberries,
  drained
¼ cup kirsch
½ teaspoon raspberry extract
1 quart heavy cream, whipped

Cook the sugar and water until it reaches 240 degrees on a candy thermometer. Pour the syrup over the egg yolks in a mixing bowl and beat to mix well. Add the raspberry jam. Then stir in the raspberries, kirsch, and raspberry extract. Mix with the whipped cream, cover, and refrigerate.
Makes 6 to 8 servings.

★

Now, try a little tidbit from Nick's Fish Market in Chicago. Their catfish fillet is out of this world—and can be finished off nicely with a dish of their Lucien Cream.

☆ Lucien Cream ☆

1¼ cups sugar
¾ cup water
1¼ tablespoons unflavored
  gelatin

1½ cups heavy cream
2½ cups sour cream
1¼ teaspoons vanilla extract
½ teaspoon rose water

Bring the sugar and water to a boil. Lower the heat and whip in gelatin. Remove from the heat.
In a large bowl, mix together the remaining ingredients. Stir in the sugar-water mixture. Pour into individual molds or one large mold, cover, and refrigerate for at least 2 hours. Remove from the mold to serve, and, if you like, top with fresh berries of the season.
Makes 6 servings.

Just Desserts

★

Finally, imagine that you're driving east, toward the Atlantic Ocean in south Georgia. You head out over the water on a causeway. First, you're struck by the marshes, the waving sea oats, and the glimmering water. Then, before you know it, you've entered paradise.

This is Sea Island, Georgia, one of a series of beautiful little islands just off the coast which have some of the greatest resorts and restaurants in the world. One of my favorites is the Cloister on Sea Island.

The first time I ever went to the Cloister was after our family had spent some time down in Orlando, Florida, fighting one of the biggest crowds that had ever visited Disney World. On the drive up north toward Georgia, we were all so hot and tired that I thought I was going to faint. I'm not one of those people who can go on a fast. I have to eat regularly, or I feel as though I'm in danger of dying!

As we left the mainland and drove onto the Sea Island paradise where the Cloister is located, you can just picture the way we looked: There were cookie crumbs, potato chip bags, and soda bottles littering the floor of our car. To make matters worse, we were wearing the same clothes we had been dressed in for several days. I hadn't even shaved; and to top it all off, we didn't have reservations.

"Mary, they proably won't even let us in this place!" I told my wife. "But you look better than any of us, why don't you go in and see if you can get a room."

Sure enough, they were almost booked solid, but Mary managed to get us accommodations just outside of the main hotel area.

That was the beginning of my rehabilitation from our holiday, my return to the world of the living. We immediately began to relax on their beautiful beach, to stroll along their palm-shaded walkways, and to be rejuvenated by their wonderful food. I was so happy I bought my first bottle of Dom Perignon champagne—an impulse decision which set me back quite a few bucks.

When I first saw their selection of desserts, I literally couldn't make a decision, so I took several! Let me give you the same option with this special "dessert tray" from the magnificent Cloister.

☆ **Cloister Banana Bisque** ☆

---

2 large ripe bananas, peeled   2 cups milk
2 tablespoons Galliano   Pinch of salt

47

Place all ingredients in a blender and purée. Chill thoroughly!

Serve the bisque in prechilled bowls or in bowls on ice, with decorative pieces of cinnamon toast on the side. Garnish the bisque with mint leaves and toasted almonds.

To make the cinnamon toast, toast 1 to 2 slices of white bread. Brush clarified butter on both sides. Sprinkle the top of the toast liberally with cinnamon sugar (in a ratio of 1 teaspoon cinnamon to 10 teaspoons sugar). Let the toast sit for a few minutes. Then bake in a very hot oven for 1 to 2 minutes. While the toast is still hot, trim off the crusts with a sharp knife and cut into small decorative triangles, squares, or hearts. Do not stack the toast while hot or it will get soggy. A wire rack would be ideal for this purpose.

Makes 4 to 6 servings.

This torte from the Cloister tastes tantalizingly similar to its namesake, the Almond Joy candy bar!

☆ Almond Joy Torte ☆

1 baked and cooled 9-inch rich chocolate cake layer (Use your favorite recipe for a chocolate layer cake or any good commercial mix.)

12 ounces finely shredded (macaroon) coconut

1¼ cups plus 2 tablespoons light corn syrup

1 cup vanilla buttercream icing (Use your favorite recipe for buttercream icing.)

Chocolate Fudge Icing (recipe follows)

Toasted sliced almonds

Cut the chocolate layer into three layers. Mix the coconut, corn syrup, and buttercream icing together and spread the mixture equally between the layers of the cake. Refrigerate while preparing the Chocolate Fudge Icing. When the icing is ready, cover the entire cake and decorate the sides and top with toasted sliced almonds.

Makes 10 to 15 servings.

☆ Chocolate Fudge Icing ☆

7 1-ounce squares unsweetened
   chocolate
5 tablespoons sugar
1¼ cups water

¼ cup (½ stick) butter
½ cup light corn syrup
5 tablespoons evaporated milk
1 teaspoon vanilla extract

Put the chocolate, sugar, water, butter, and corn syrup in a saucepan and cook to 236 degrees on a candy thermometer. Remove from the heat and cool. Add the milk gradually, while beating for approximately 10 minutes. Stir in the vanilla extract.

☆ The Cloister's Sea Island Chocolate Mousse ☆

3 cups heavy cream
1 ounce unflavored gelatin
¼ cup hot water
4 cups or 8 4.25-ounce cans
   chocolate fudge snack
   pudding
5 1-ounce squares unsweetened
   chocolate, melted

¾ pint chocolate ice cream
1½ cups large egg whites
   (approximately 12)
¼ cup sugar
¼ cup Grand Marnier
¼ cup dark rum

Whip the cream until soft peaks form and then refrigerate it.

Dissolve the gelatin in the hot water in the top of a double boiler over simmering water, stirring it from time to time until it's completely smooth.

In a large bowl, combine the chocolate pudding, melted gelatin, and melted chocolate with a spoon or spatula.

Add the ice cream in small pieces and blend well.

Fold in the whipped cream, using a wire whisk.

Beat the egg whites at high speed until soft peaks form, adding the sugar gradually.

Fold the beaten egg whites into the chocolate mixture; add Grand Marnier and rum. Be careful not to overmix. When completely blended, pour the mousse into a bowl, smooth the top with a spatula, cover, and refrigerate. Chill for at least five hours before serving.
Makes 12 servings.

☆ The Cloister's Peach Charlotte ☆
(Or Peach Mousse, if served from a bowl)

1¾ cups heavy cream
¾ ounce unflavored gelatin
¼ cup hot water
4 cups vanilla custard, or 4 4.25-ounce cans vanilla snack pudding
¼ cup brandy (or more), or brandy flavoring

¾ cup vanilla ice cream
4 large egg whites
¼ cup sugar
2 drained canned peach halves, or more, if desired, diced and soaked in brandy
Whipped cream and sliced peaches for garnish

Whip the cream until soft peaks form and then refrigerate it.

Dissolve the gelatin in hot water in the top of a double boiler over simmering water, stirring a few times.

In a large bowl, combine the custard, melted gelatin, and brandy with a spatula. Add the ice cream in small pieces and blend it in with spatula or with an electric mixer. Fold in the whipped cream with a wire whisk.

Beat the egg whites at high speed until soft peaks form, adding the sugar gradually. Fold the diced peaches and beaten egg whites into the custard mixture until all is totally blended. Pour into a 1½-quart bowl and refrigerate for several hours or overnight.

To remove the mousse from the bowl, hold the bowl completely in warm water until the mousse loosens from the sides; turn it upside down over a serving plate. A little shaking and patting will help to overcome the suction and the Charlotte will come out of the bowl. Shortly before serving, the Charlotte should be decorated with whipped cream and sliced peaches.

Makes 8 to 10 servings.

☆ Rum and Plum Pot ☆

1 pound fresh plums (For canned plums see Variation.)
1 cup sugar
4 cups water
1 vanilla bean, split

½ teaspoon ground cinnamon
½ teaspoon ground allspice
2 cups dark rum, more or less to taste

Wash the plums and cut them in half; then remove the pits. Combine the sugar and water in a saucepan and bring to a boil. Poach the plums in the sugar water. Then add the vanilla bean, cinnamon, and allspice. Cover and chill thoroughly.

Remove the vanilla bean and purée the plums and cooking liquid in a blender. Add the rum. Adjust the flavorings by adding lemon juice if it is too sweet or sugar if it is too tart. Pour into a bowl and refrigerate for at least 24 hours to set—this improves the flavor. Keep chilled until ready to serve.
Makes 10 to 12 servings.

VARIATION: Remove the pits from one #10 can of plums; add the plums and juice to 1 pint of rum. Sprinkle in the cinnamon and allspice. Chill and let set for a few days. Then purée in a blender. Adjust the flavorings as above.

Note: Both fresh and canned Rum Plum Pot may be thinned out with a little pineapple juice, if necessary.

☆ Turkish Cassata ☆

1 tablespoon boiling water	1 cup chopped pecans
1 tablespoon instant coffee powder	½ cup rich chocolate sauce
2 quarts coffee ice cream, softened	1 9-inch sponge or pound cake layer (see Note)

Add the boiling water to the coffee powder, dissolve and let cool. Put the coffee ice cream into a mixing bowl. Add the coffee and beat at medium speed until light and fluffy. Line the bottom of a 9-inch spring-form pan with a sheet of paper and cover with half the pecans.

Carefully spread half of the ice cream on top of the pecans, filling the pan halfway up. Then sprinkle the remaining pecans evenly on top of the ice cream. With a tablespoon pour and spread the chocolate sauce over the nuts.

Cover all with the remaining ice cream and smooth the top to an even surface with a spatula. Put a ½-inch-thick slice of sponge or pound cake on top. Cover and place in the freezer until frozen solid.

To serve, put the pan upside down on a plate, open and remove the

sides and bottom of the pan. The cassata is ready for cutting with a knife (which should be dipped in hot water). As an added touch, serve it with a generous portion of a light-colored butterscotch sauce.
Makes 8 to 10 servings.

Note: Use your favorite recipe for a sponge or pound cake or any good commercial mix.

☆ The Cloister's Pecan Pie ☆

9 large eggs
1¾ cups granulated sugar or packed dark brown sugar
4 cups dark corn syrup
1 tablespoon vanilla extract

1 teaspoon salt
1 cup (2 sticks) butter, melted
3 cups pecan pieces
2 half-baked 9-inch frozen pie shells

Preheat the oven to 350 degrees. Beat eggs, sugar, corn syrup, vanilla, and salt slightly with a wire whisk. Do not overmix. To avoid foaming, strain through a fine sieve into a clean bowl and add the melted butter.

Spread the pecans in the half-baked pie shells and pour the mixture evenly over them. (The custard should come halfway up.) Stir with a spoon to assure an even filling. Then put the pies into the oven and pour more of the mixture up to the rim of the pie shell. Make sure the shell stands level.

Bake for about 20 minutes; then lower the oven temperature to 300 degrees and continue baking for another 20 minutes. Since ovens bake differently, check to see whether the edges of the filling are baking much faster than the center. If this is the case, remove the pie from the oven and let the high edges deflate to the level of the rest of the pie. Then continue until completely baked. Be careful not to overbake. (A pecan pie gives you the best taste of its wonderful ingredients when it's on the *soft* side, especially when it is served cold.)
Makes 12 to 16 servings.

★

There are probably more fine restaurants per square mile on Captiva Island, Florida than anywhere else in the world. Here's a tasty dessert from Timmy's Nook, one of Captiva's most popular eating spots.

☆ Blueberry Sour Cream Pie ☆

1 cup sugar
¼ cup all-purpose flour
½ teaspoon salt
2 cups sour cream
2 large eggs

¾ teaspoon almond extract
1 9-inch graham cracker pie
   shell
1 can blueberry pie filling

Preheat the oven to 350 degrees. Combine the first 6 ingredients in a mixing bowl. Beat by hand until well mixed. Pour into the pie shell. Bake for 30 to 35 minutes, or until set in the middle. Top the hot pie with the blueberries. Cool, cover, and chill. Serve, topped with Cool Whip.
Makes 6 to 8 servings.

☆ 3 ☆

Willard's All-American Seafood Fantasies

It's always hard to pick an "all-American team"—whether you're talking about football or food.

Still, after you've visited hundreds of cities and dined in thousands of restaurants around the country as I have over the past few decades, certain candidates for the all-American "first team" of food begin to emerge. In this section, I want to focus on the tastiest, most exquisite seafood entrées I've encountered in my travels.

Certainly, there are plenty of fine seafood courses other than the ones I've included which are tantalizing the taste buds of many people throughout the country. So I've had to make some hard decisions in coming up with this roster of first-rate dishes.

But I think that among these entrées you'll find some of the crown jewels of the deep that have ended up on the tables of the country's best dining rooms. As you'll see, no single part of the nation has a corner on the first team of fine foods. Massachusetts, Florida, Oregon, Illinois— you can look into almost any corner of this great land of ours and find some succulent something that will satisfy your most exotic food fantasies.

★

Legal Sea Foods Inc. has six restaurant locations in the Boston area —and well they might. Legal is truly a Boston *and* national landmark as far as seafood is concerned.

Roger S. Berkowitz, the head honcho at Legal Sea Foods, likes to tell this little story about his establishment:

"One of my favorite stories concerns a gentleman who came into our restaurant to 'break out of his diet.' He proceeded to consume a plate of oysters, a hearty dish called Baked Mussels au Gratin, smoked bluefish pâté, six grilled jumbo shrimp—and that was only his appetizer.

"For his main course, he had a four-and-a-half-pound lobster, and then he really outdid himself on our desserts. He practically inhaled a salad-dish-sized bowl of homemade ice cream. And if that weren't enough, he topped it all off with a hot fudge sundae!

"The guest? Willard Scott, who else? He now ranks right at the top of Legal Sea Foods' all-time customers."

To give you some idea about how fantastic this diet-breaking adventure of mine was, here are a couple of the dishes that did it: the Baked Mussels au Gratin and Smoked Bluefish Pâté. Although this fine restaurant offers every variety of seafood dish, these two are so special that they serve to set Legal Sea Foods off from all the rest.

☆ Baked Mussels au Gratin ☆

60 to 72 mussels	2 cups seasoned cracker crumbs
3 cups (6 sticks) butter, softened	1 cup (2 sticks) butter, melted
3 tablespoons minced garlic	1 pound Monterey Jack cheese,
3 tablespoons chopped parsley	grated

Clean and wash the mussels. Discard any that do not close when handled.

Steam the mussels just until they open; then cool under cool running water. Separate the two shells of each mussel, retaining the shell half with the meat. Preheat the oven to 425 degrees.

Blend the softened butter, garlic, and parsley together in a bowl.

In a separate bowl, blend the cracker crumbs and melted butter together.

Arrange 10 to 12 steamed mussels in individual baking pans. Make sure the pans have raised edges to retain any melted butter which might spill from the shells. Top each mussel with 1 teaspoon of the garlic butter, a generous portion of grated Monterey Jack cheese, and a sprinkle of seasoned cracker crumbs.

Bake until the crumbs are brown and the cheese has melted.
Makes 6 servings.

☆ Smoked Bluefish Pâté ☆

If you like a densely flavored pâté, use this recipe. For a lighter version, try the variation.

1 pound smoked bluefish fillets
4 ounces cream cheese, softened
3 tablespoons butter, softened
2 tablespoons Cognac
1 tablespoon minced onion

¼ to ½ teaspoon Worcestershire
  sauce
1 tablespoon lemon juice
Salt and freshly ground black
  pepper

Whirl the bluefish, cream cheese, butter, and Cognac in a food processor until smooth. Add the onion, Worcestershire sauce, and lemon juice and pulse the machine on and off until the ingredients are combined. Taste and adjust the seasonings with salt and pepper.

Pack into a crock and serve with crackers or thinly sliced pieces of toast. The pâté will keep in the refrigerator for 4 to 5 days; it may also be frozen for up to 3 months.
Makes about 3¼ cups.

VARIATION: This variation uses a greater proportion of cream cheese and seasonings. Prepare as above. Makes about 4 cups.

1 pound smoked bluefish fillets
1 8-ounce package cream
  cheese, softened
¼ cup (½ stick) butter, softened
3 tablespoons minced onion

2 tablespoons lemon juice
½ teaspoon Worcestershire
  sauce
Salt and freshly ground black
  pepper

★

As I've said, I know there are many, many wonderful restaurants in this country which we haven't included in this cookbook. In the last analysis, the recipes you'll find in these pages represent a personal "Scott selection," based on my own peculiar taste and preferences. But having offered this qualification, I must say that I think Jake's in Portland, Oregon, would have to be placed toward the top of anyone's list.

Here, then, are five super seafood specialties from Jake's.

☆ Stark Street Sturgeon ☆

7 ounces sturgeon fillet	1 tablespoon butter
Salt	6 to 8 fresh basil leaves, coarsely
¼ tablespoon cracked black	chopped
peppercorns	1 tablespoon Dijon mustard
All-purpose flour	2 tablespoons water, or as
1 tablespoon vegetable oil	needed

Season sturgeon with salt and pepper; then dust with the flour. Heat a frying pan over medium-high heat and add the oil. Once the oil is hot, add the sturgeon. Cook until slightly browned on both sides. Remove the sturgeon to a warm plate and wipe the pan clean with paper towels. Add the butter, basil, and mustard. Cook, stirring, for 20 to 30 seconds; add water, stir, and remove from the heat. If the sauce is not homogeneous, add a touch more water.

Pour the sauce over the sturgeon and garnish with additional fresh basil leaves.

Makes 2 servings.

☆ Crawfish McCall ☆

1½ tablespoons finely chopped	4 to 5 ounces béchamel sauce
onion	(page 147)
1 tablespoon butter	2 to 4 tablespoons heavy cream
¼ cup small fresh morels	¼ pound cooked crawfish tails
¼ cup pitted fresh cherries	Cayenne pepper to taste
1 tablespoon julienned orange	1 tablespoon whipped cream
peel, blanched	Pinch of chopped parsley
1 teaspoon grated ginger root	Salt and pepper to taste

In a 10-inch frying pan, sauté the onion in the butter until translucent. Add the morels and cook for approximately 10 to 15 seconds. (Do not brown the onion. Moisten with water if necessary.) Add the cherries and cook for approximately 15 to 20 seconds. Add the orange peel and ginger and cook for 10 seconds. Add the béchamel and heavy cream. Lower the heat and cook to the desired consistency. Add crawfish tails and cayenne and cook until the crawfish are hot (not longer than 15 to 20 seconds). *(Continued)*

Fold in the tablespoon of whipped cream. Add the parsley and season with salt and pepper to taste. Serve with Oriental Rice with Almonds. *Makes 2 to 4 servings.*

☆ Oriental Rice with Almonds ☆

Grated rind of 1 lemon
1 teaspoon butter
¼ cup finely chopped toasted
  almonds

1 cup *cooked* rice (Oriental
  preferred)
Pinch of chopped parsley
Salt and pepper to taste

Sauté the lemon rind in the butter. Add the almonds, rice, and parsley. Toss. Season with salt and pepper to taste.

Press into a mold and place in the center of a platter. Remove the mold and spoon any seafood dish, such as Crawfish McCall, gently around the molded rice.
Makes 2 to 4 servings.

☆ Crawfish Allison ☆

8 to 12 cooked crawfish, tail
  shells removed and tails still
  intact
1½ tablespoons butter
1 tablespoon Dijon mustard

1 tablespoon honey
Pinch of cayenne pepper
1 tablespoon chopped scallion
  tops

Heat the crawfish in a frying pan with 1 tablespoon of the butter. Remove the crawfish when they are hot. Add the Dijon mustard, honey, cayenne pepper, remaining butter, and chopped scallion tops to the pan. Return the crawfish to the pan and toss in the sauce. Remove the crawfish and arrange them around a platter with tails pointed inward to the center. Pour the sauce over the crawfish and garnish the center of platter as desired.
Makes 4 to 6 servings.

☆ Crawfish Cascadia ☆

½ tablespoon finely chopped
  onion
6 ounces chanterelles, sliced
1 tablespoon dry white wine
6 ounces cooked crawfish tails
1 tablespoon brandy
2 tablespoons crawfish sauce
  (bisque)
2 tablespoons béchamel sauce
  (page 147)

⅛ teaspoon saffron threads
1 tablespoon Dijon mustard
¾ to 1 tablespoon grated
  Gruyère cheese
¼ teaspoon chopped parsley
Pinch of cayenne pepper
1 teaspoon heavy cream
1 teaspoon hollandaise sauce
  (page 147)
Salt and pepper to taste

Cook the onion, chanterelles, and white wine together in a frying pan for approximately 45 to 60 seconds. Add the crawfish tails and brandy. Ignite the brandy with a long kitchen match. When the flames subside, add the crawfish and béchamel sauce, saffron, Dijon mustard, cheese, and parsley and mix well. Then add the cayenne pepper, heavy cream, and hollandaise. Season with salt and pepper to taste and serve.
Makes 1 to 2 servings.

Willard tackles a profusion of underwater delights at The Sea Captain's House in Myrtle Beach, South Carolina. (Photo courtesy of Joye B. Nesbitt/W. Edward Clement, II)

★

The Sea Captain's House in Myrtle Beach, South Carolina, has more fantastic fish dishes than you can shake a fishing pole at. In fact, the place has become so popular since it was founded in 1962 that they've had to increase the seating capacity steadily to its present size of 180 seats.

In my usual inimitable fashion, I was so overcome by this garden of underwater delights that I outdid myself (even by more than usual) at the dinner table.

They started me off with an entrée-size appetizer of Sea Island Shrimp. The sandy, coastal barrier islands of the Carolinas and Georgia are famous for their profusion of fresh seafood, including shrimp, which grow in the shallows, inlets, and briny backwaters. Prior to the days of refrigeration, early settlers enjoyed the abundance of shrimp caught among these sea islands. Furthermore, because fresh seafood is very perishable before and after being cooked, these shrimpers devised recipes for extending the edible life of the seafood.

For example, to keep boiled shrimp from spoiling too quickly, the old-timers would marinate the little creatures in oil and vinegar, and also add spices and herbs for seasoning. The Sea Captain's House recipe

for Sea Island Shrimp comes from one of these early American recipes
—and that's how I got started on my seafood saga that evening.

☆ Sea Island Shrimp ☆

SHRIMP
5 pounds just-cooked shrimp
(boiled lightly)
10 white onions, sliced and
separated into thin rings

DRESSING
2 cups olive or vegetable oil
1¾ cups good quality cider
vinegar
1 16-oz bottle capers, including
liquid
Salt, sugar, Tabasco sauce, and
Worcestershire sauce to taste

In a deep flat pan, place a layer of shrimp, then a layer of onion slices,
alternating until all ingredients are used up.

Combine the dressing ingredients and mix well.

Pour the dressing over the shrimp and onions. Cover with aluminum
foil and refrigerate for *at least 12 hours before serving.*

To serve, lift the shrimp and onions out of the dressing and place on
a large platter. Decorate with crisp lettuce leaves.
Makes 10 to 12 servings.

★

After that huge helping of Sea Island Shrimp, I wasn't sure I'd be able
to eat anything else, but then, the Sea Captain's staff served me their
Low Country Crab Casserole—and I was off on another Carolina seafood
adventure. In fact, it was so good, I actually asked for a second helping!

There's an interesting story, too, behind why this Low Country Crab
Casserole is so excellent. It means that for many years a popular restaurant called The Pink House was operated in Myrtle Beach by one Leroy
Letts. One of his most popular entrées was a low country crab casserole
which used the white crab meat found in abundance most of the year
along the South Carolina coast.

When Letts discontinued the operation of The Pink House, the newly-
founded Sea Captain's House Restaurant hired one of their chefs, Willie
Nivens—for the sole purpose of securing this crab recipe. But as it
turned out, the Sea Captain's House got more than the recipe. Nivens

became an extremely valuable employee who contributed much to the restaurant's success for more than twenty years, until his death just a couple of years ago.

☆ Low Country Crab Casserole ☆

4 large eggs
2 tablespoons margarine, softened
1 tablespoon chopped chives
½ cup mayonnaise
½ cup dry bread crumbs

6 tablespoons milk
Salt and pepper to taste
1 pound lump crab meat, picked over and shells removed
Pinch of paprika
Dash of dry sherry

Preheat the oven to 425 degrees. Whip the eggs in a mixing bowl using a wire whisk. Add the remaining ingredients *except* the crab meat, paprika, and sherry. Mix well. Add the crab meat and mix well.

Butter 4 individual ovenproof casserole dishes. Put the crab mixture into the dishes and sprinkle with paprika. Bake for 12 minutes, or until golden brown and spongy to the touch. Remove and sprinkle with sherry.

Makes 4 servings.

★

After that second casserole, I was absolutely sure I was finished. But just as I was about to get up, they placed before me the Coastal Crab Broil au Gratin. I thought, "I'll never make it through this! I'm filled to the gills!"

Before I realized it, however, the tantalizing aroma of that Crab Broil had tempted me to put a little touch of it into my mouth—and I was on my way again.

One of the things that really grabbed me about the Coastal Crab Broil au Gratin was the incredible combination of cheese and blue crab white meat. As it happens, that's the essence of the secret of this recipe.

Before the Sea Captain's House opened, almost 25 years ago, one of the aspiring owners, who was especially fond of cheese, began looking for unusual and tasty recipes. As far as he was concerned, the more cheese the better. Also, like me, he loved fresh white meat from blue crabs, especially when it was very lightly seasoned.

When he came across a California recipe which combined crab meat on toast with melted cheese, this founding father of the restaurant devised his special version of Coastal Crab Broil au Gratin. His goal all along had been the best for any restaurateur—to satisfy his own appetite for crab and cheese.

This guy really had hit the mark as far as I was concerned. And I'm happy to report that I savored this dish as much as I had the two previous ones—and even went on to polish off a dessert!

☆ Coastal Crab Broil au Gratin ☆

2 pounds crab meat, picked over
   and flaked
½ cup mayonnaise
1 teaspoon Worcestershire sauce
½ teaspoon lemon juice

Dash of Tabasco sauce
16 slices bread, lightly toasted
Shredded sharp natural Cheddar
   cheese to taste

Combine all the ingredients *except* the bread and cheese. For each serving, spread 2 slices of lightly toasted bread generously with the mixture.

Sprinkle with the shredded cheese and broil only until the cheese has melted.

Makes 8 servings.

★

The first time I ever went to Detroit, it was to attend the Republican National Convention in 1980, at which Ronald Reagan was nominated for President. While there, I went to the London Chop House with two of my favorite friends in the whole world, Pat Buchanan and Tom Braden.

Although I had appeared on their cable television show *Crossfire,* my relationship with these two guys goes back much further. Among other things, we worked together on radio in Washington, D.C. During my last appearance on their *Crossfire* program, just before Buchanan moved into the Reagan administration to become the White House Director of Communications, I let them take potshots at me for dressing up on network television as "Carmen Miranda."

The night we all trekked over to the London Chop House in Detroit, I ordered several popular lake fish dishes, including walleyed pike (the first time for me) and some incredibly tasty lake trout. I've always preferred freshwater to saltwater fish, and it's hard to find a better place for the freshwater variety than Detroit's London Chop House.

The London Chop House also has this great, old-fashioned bar, which has all the accoutrements that a bar aficionado could want. For one thing, it features Stroh's Signature Beer, in my opinion the finest brew made in the United States. Sitting right up on the bar is a tray of egg holders with some tasty hard-boiled eggs which patrons can have as an appetizer.

The beautiful wood interior of this place is ready-made to make a smoked fish dish like this lake trout recipe reach a peak of culinary perfection.

☆ Smoked Lake Trout Fillets with Horseradish ☆

SAUCE
2 large egg yolks
3 tablespoons lemon juice
2 tablespoons Dijon mustard
½ teaspoon salt
¼ teaspoon pepper
¼ teaspoon Tabasco sauce
½ cup corn oil

8 lemon wedges

GARNISH
4 ounces golden whitefish caviar
8 watercress sprigs
½ cup olive oil
½ cup drained prepared horseradish
½ cup chopped watercress

8 4-ounce smoked lake trout fillets

To make the sauce, combine the egg yolks, lemon juice, mustard, salt, pepper, and Tabasco sauce in a bowl. Beat with an electric mixer to combine. Slowly add the oils while beating. Mix in the horseradish and watercress. Cover and refrigerate until cold.

To prepare the trout, remove the skin from the fillets. Scrape off the dark fatty tissue from under the skin. Remove the bones with needle-nose pliers.

To serve, spoon ¼ cup of the sauce into the center of each plate. Lay the trout on top of the sauce. Spoon a tablespoon of caviar onto each trout fillet. Garnish each serving with a sprig of watercress and a lemon wedge.
Makes 8 servings.

Now, here is the London Chop House's special preparation for northern pike.

☆ Grilled Northern Pike with Vermouth ☆

3 cups fish fumet
1 pound pike bones or head
¼ cup chopped shallots
1½ cups dry vermouth
16 to 20 whole garlic cloves, peeled
16 to 20 whole shallots, peeled
3 tablespoons unsalted butter
4 9-ounce northern pike steaks

¼ cup (½ stick) unsalted butter, melted
1 cup crème fraîche, or ½ cup heavy cream mixed with ½ cup sour cream
Thinly sliced green tops of 1 bunch of scallions
1 bunch chives, diced
Salt and pepper to taste

Combine the fish fumet, pike bones, chopped shallots, and 1¼ cups of the vermouth in a stainless steel or enameled saucepan. Bring to a simmer over medium heat and simmer for 25 minutes. Remove the pike bones with a slotted spoon. Continue to cook until reduced to ¾ cup. Remove from the heat. Immediately strain through a very fine sieve and set aside.

Meanwhile, sauté the whole garlic and shallots in the 3 tablespoons of butter over medium heat. Season very lightly with salt. Turn the heat to low, add the remaining vermouth, cover, and cook until tender. Remove from the heat and set aside.

Preheat the broiler to 425 degrees. Position the broiler pan approximately 4 inches from the heat source.

Brush the pike steaks on both sides with the melted butter. Place the steaks on the broiler pan and broil for 8 to 10 minutes.

Meanwhile, return the reduced fumet-sauce base to a simmer. Add the crème fraîche. Reduce over medium heat to the consistency of a light sauce. Add the whole garlic and shallots and season with salt and pepper. Add the scallions and the chives and remove from the heat.

Remove the pike steaks from the broiler and quickly remove the skin and backbone with a paring knife; remove the side bones with needle-nose pliers. Put the steaks on a warm serving platter. Spoon some sauce over the steaks and evenly divide the garlic and shallot garnish among the steaks.

Makes 4 servings.

★

Now, let's shift back to a specialty of Joe's Stone Crab Restaurant in Miami Beach.

Joe's, by the way, is located on the southern tip of Miami Beach. Established in 1913, two years before Miami Beach itself was incorporated, the restaurant still occupies its original site. Because Joe's is a historic landmark on Miami Beach, most taxi drivers will know where it's located, but if you need to help out with directions, just tell your driver that upon crossing any of the bridges from mainland Miami to Miami Beach, you turn south and ride to the dead end.

☆ Seviche ☆

1 pound scallops	1 teaspoon salt
1 bunch scallions, chopped	2 tablespoons chopped sweet
1 cup lime juice	green pepper
½ cup orange juice	4 tablespoons chopped parsley
6 tablespoons chopped onion	½ cup olive oil
Pinch of crushed red pepper	Dash of Tabasco sauce
flakes	Pinch of ground pepper
½ teaspoon dried oregano	

Combine the scallops, scallions, lime juice, and orange juice. Toss well, cover, and refrigerate for 3 to 4 hours. Drain and add the remaining ingredients. Toss well.
Makes 3 to 4 servings.

★

The Charcoal Grill in Milwaukee boasts that it's the "Home of the World's Longest Shishkabob—82 feet, 4 inches." They're not so bad on oysters, either. One specialty of theirs, Grilled Oysters with Radish Dressing, has been one of the finalists in the National Oyster Cook-Off in Leonardtown, Maryland.

The Grill's Victoria Fabiano nominates oysters as the national food because, she reminds us, "Oysters stimulate *romance!* Your favorite topic and mine!"

Pearl or no pearl—oysters are always among Willard's favorite crown jewels of the deep. (Photo courtesy of Frank Taylor II)

☆ The Charcoal Grill's Grilled Oysters ☆ With Radish Dressing

12 oysters in the shell
2 tablespoons grated red radish
1 teaspoon soy sauce
2 tablespoons rice vinegar

2 tablespoons fresh lemon juice
½ teaspoon grated lemon rind
Minced fresh chives, to taste

Put the oysters in a hinged grill and set over hot coals. Cook until they open, about 5 to 10 minutes. Combine the radish, soy sauce, rice vinegar, lemon juice, and lemon rind. Pour the dressing over the oysters. Sprinkle lightly with minced chives and serve at once.
Makes 2 to 3 servings.

★

The Greenbrier in White Sulphur Springs, West Virginia, is perhaps the premier old-fashioned resort "in the grand style" in America. The

67

service is without equal; and the setting is splendid in those spectacular wooded mountains which are part of the Appalachian chain. There's plenty of opportunity to work up an appetite there, with hiking trails, carriage rides, and practically every other form of outdoor activity.

Once you enter this special place, you find yourself taking a couple of steps backward into American history. Tradition has it that the Greenbrier was the first place that General Robert E. Lee visited after the Civil War ended. He was invited by the Greenbrier's management in a public-spirited gesture to help heal the rift that had developed in the country during the war.

West Virginia, of course, had split off from Virginia because of strong Union sentiments. Yet the area had strong enough ties to the South to put it in a position to act as a bridge between the North and the South after peace was reestablished. In addition to a reputation for public service, the Greenbrier was right on a railroad line, a fact which helped bring in the customers despite its secluded location.

There are a couple of additional things that make the Greenbrier especially outstanding today. The first is the expertise of the manager, Bill Pitt, who epitomizes the Greenbrier's tradition of great food service. The second is their marvelous buffet lunch—certainly one of the tastiest. and most impressive in the entire world.

I'm also particularly partial to this place because it's only one stop-light from my house in Virginia! I can get on Route 81 and drive to Route 64, and then I only run into one stoplight during the entire 200-mile trip.

There are still plenty of touches of the past at the Greenbrier, including a violin at dinnertime and daily afternoon tea. At the same time, with the modern tennis courts, golf courses, and other facilities, there's everything that any person could want in the way of modern conveniences. The place even makes its own chocolates and boasts a chocolate shop which is second to none.

But now, let's get down to the specifics of their food. They've provided us with some of their "charcutiere specialties"—some seafood dishes which require special marinades and smoking techniques. But first of all, we need to understand exactly what the Greenbrier's procedures are for home curing, drying, and smoking.

Home Curing

Curing is the key to the smoking process. Salt is the major ingredient, though sugar, herbs, pepper, and garlic are also commonly used.

Curing enhances the texture and flavor of a food by drawing out moisture. This concentrates the flavor and firms the texture of items such as trout. Curing also extends the shelf life of a product because the presence of salt and the loss of moisture slows the bacterial process.

Certain brining processes may require a rinse to remove the salt and herbs from the surface. Rinse lightly in cool water and then set the food on a rack to dry.

Home Drying

Another important and most overlooked aspect of smoking is the drying process. Smoke won't adhere to a wet surface, so the items must be air-dried to develop a full smoke flavor. Drying also increases eye appeal by the formation of a pellicle, which is the thin, glossy, transparent layer on the top of many smoked foods.

Items can be air-dried in a cool room or for a longer period of time in the refrigerator. Dry the items until there's no visible moisture and the items start to feel a little sticky to the touch. But don't over-dry, as this will create a dry and tough final product.

Home Smoking

For home purposes, smoking and cooking should take place at the same time in a process known as "hot smoking."

This can be achieved in a charcoal grill with a tight-fitting cover or in any of the small smokers on the market for home smoking. If you're using a purchased smoker, follow the manufacturer's instructions. When using a charcoal grill, add the wood chips to the burning charcoal briquettes.

Place the food on the racks, cover, and cook. Grapevines, woods such as apple, hickory, maple, or mesquite, and corncobs can all be used for smoking. In general, any hardwood tree that loses its leaves in the winter is good for smoking, and any tree that bears needles is not. Wood can be used green or dry, but if the wood is too dry, it may need to be soaked in water to get the maximum amount of smoke and the least amount of flames.

Finally, try to minimize the heat loss by not opening the cooker too often so the product will have enough exposure to the smoke to develop the desired flavor.

And now, for the food! These recipes, provided by Rodney Stoner, the Greenbrier's executive food director, can be made in the home smokers which are available commercially. Also, if you want to make smaller amounts than those indicated, just reduce the ingredients proportionately.

☆ Whitefish Marinade ☆

1 cup salt
Juice of 8 lemons
5 pounds whitefish fillets

1 gallon water
1 bunch fresh dill

Combine all ingredients. Marinate the whitefish fillets—1 per person—overnight. Smoke.
Makes 15 servings.

☆ Scallops ☆

1½ pounds scallops
½ cup honey
2 garlic cloves
12 juniper berries

2 cups vegetable oil
2 bay leaves
1 teaspoon fresh thyme leaves

Combine all the ingredients. Marinate overnight. Smoke with hickory chips.
Makes 6 to 8 servings.

☆ Shrimp ☆

5 pounds raw shrimp, shelled
1¼ cups cold water
¼ cup packed dark brown sugar
¼ cup lemon juice

5 cups ice
1¼ cups kosher salt
½ teaspoon garlic powder
½ teaspoon onion powder

Combine all the ingredients. Cure for 1 hour. Cold smoke for 3 hours. Hot smoke to cook.
Makes 15 to 20 servings.

☆ Smoked Trout ☆

3 cups salt	1½ cups sugar
½ teaspoon garlic powder	½ teaspoon white pepper
½ teaspoon ground cumin	½ teaspoon ground mace
½ teaspoon dried marjoram	3 to 4 pounds trout fillets

Combine all the ingredients and cover the trout fillets with the mixture. Let sit for 45 minutes. Rinse lightly with cold water. Cold smoke for 3 hours. Hot smoke to cook.
Makes 10 servings.

★

Most people who are unfamiliar with rural American customs don't know much about the tradition of country ham, especially Virginia ham. In Tidewater, Virginia, where most of the early colonists settled, you're in the heart of peanut country. In many cases, those peanuts are fed to the hogs, and the results are nothing short of phenomenal. The meat that you get from those pigs is as lean, red, and tasty as you'll find anywhere. Also, that part of Virginia has a perfect temperature for curing hams. The ideal temperature tends to be from just above freezing to between 35 and 45 degrees.

But ham is often only part of the story when it comes to authentic Tidewater cooking. All along the Chesapeake Bay and the James and York rivers, you'll find a bountiful supply of hard-shell crabs. (The real name is the Chesapeake Bay Blue Crab.)

What this adds up to in Virginia kitchens is a magnificent combination of ham and crab meat—a special American creation discovered by our forefathers which has to rank as one of the great taste sensations of all time. The marriage of crab meat to Virginia ham is so incredibly complementary that it's impossible to put the delight into words. To the colonists, a dish of thinly sliced Smithfield ham topped with lump crab meat was American ambrosia. Then they outdid themselves by experimenting with sauces until they found just the right flavor to bring the ham-crab meat combination to an ultimate peak.

Today, you can sample this all-American taste discovery at Colonial Williamsburg with these two recipes.

☆ Virginia Ham and Crab Cakes ☆

10 tablespoons heavy cream
1 pound crab meat, picked over
 and flaked
3 ounces Virginia ham, finely
 diced
1 large egg yolk

½ sweet red pepper, diced
½ sweet green pepper, diced
All-purpose flour
Fine dry bread crumbs
Clarified butter
Tomato Fondue Sauce (recipe
 follows)

Heat the cream in a saucepan and continue cooking until only about 2 tablespoons of thick liquid remain. Let cool. Blend all the crab meat, ham, cream, egg yolk, and peppers well in a bowl. Form into 8 to 10 flat cakes. Dust with flour and bread crumbs and sauté in the clarified butter until each side is golden brown. Serve with Tomato Fondue Sauce.
Makes 4 to 5 servings.

☆ Tomato Fondue Sauce ☆

2 tablespoons minced white
 onion
1½ teaspoons minced garlic
2 tablespoons olive oil
1½ teaspoons minced celery
1 medium carrot, diced

4 whole tomatoes, peeled,
 seeded, and diced
1½ teaspoons minced ham
¼ cup tomato purée
⅝ cup chicken broth
Salt and pepper to taste

Sauté the onion and garlic in the olive oil. Add the celery, carrots, and tomatoes. Simmer for a few minutes. Add the ham and tomato purée. Add the broth to thin to the desired consistency. Season with salt and pepper.
Makes 4 to 5 servings.

☆ Virginia Crab Meat Sauté Randolph ☆

4 frozen patty shells
8 ounces backfin crab meat
2 teaspoons lemon juice
2 tablespoons butter
2 teaspoons minced shallot

¾ cup hollandaise sauce (page 87)
2 teaspoons Dijon mustard
8 thin slices Virginia ham

Preheat the oven to 450 degrees. Place the patty shells upside down on an ungreased baking sheet. Lower the oven temperature to 400 degrees and bake for 20 minutes. Cut each shell in half, lengthwise.

Pick over the crab meat, discarding any bits of shell or cartilage. Toss the crab meat gently with the lemon juice.

Melt the butter in a small frying pan. Add the shallot and sauté over medium heat until soft. Do not brown. Add the crab meat and sauté over low heat for 2 minutes, tossing gently so that the crab meat is well coated with the butter.

Combine the hollandaise sauce and mustard. Place 2 patty shell halves on each of 4 warmed plates. Place a slice of Virginia ham on each patty shell halve and top with the crab meat. Cover the crab meat with the hollandaise sauce and serve at once.
Makes 4 servings.

★

Mobile, Alabama, claims that it was the first place in the country to have Mardi Gras, even before New Orleans. The story goes like this.

Mobile had been a major seaport during the Civil War, and, of course, it was devastated by the Union fleet. Then, by one tradition, an early promotion-minded citizen by the name of "Indian Joe" came up with the Mardi Gras in an effort to help attract some new business and get the city back on its feet economically. Another consideration was simply to generate a festive atmosphere and improve morale.

When the folks at Mobile invited me to come down for the event a few years ago, one of my hosts took me over to Wintzell's Oyster House. Located right on the Gulf, Wintzell's has a rough wooden facade and fish nets hanging all over the place. And when you sit down to that seafood bar, you know you're close to seafood heaven. They have people in the kitchen who can shuck oysters as fast as you can eat them—and they make crab cakes that are truly divine.

I arrived there about three in the afternoon, escorted by the Chief of Police of the City of Mobile and two State Troopers. We sat there for hours, eating oysters and crab meat and having the best time you can imagine.

Unfortunately, though, it had slipped my mind that I was supposed to do the local news at 5:30 P.M. The news people were going crazy looking for me all over the city. But there I was, sitting in Wintzell's, stuffing my face, with the top men in local law enforcement. And I missed the news!

☆ Baked Crabs ☆

1 large onion, minced	1 cup bread crumbs
½ cup minced celery	1 tablespoon Dijon mustard
1 small sweet green pepper, minced	1 tablespoon mayonnaise
¼ cup (½ stick) butter	2 large eggs, well beaten
1 pound light or dark crab meat, picked over	1 to 4 teaspoons garlic salt
	Salt and pepper to taste
	10 medium-size crab shells

Preheat the oven to 400 degrees. Sauté the onion, celery, and green pepper in the butter until soft but not brown. Mix the crab meat and bread crumbs together and add the sautéed vegetables along with the mustard, mayonnaise, eggs, garlic salt, and salt and pepper. Mix until well blended. Pack into the well-greased shells, sprinkle lightly with additional bread crumbs, and bake for 15 to 25 minutes, or until lightly brown. They can also be deep-fried for about 3 minutes.
Makes 5 servings.

☆ Jambalaya ☆

1 cup long-grain rice	2 garlic cloves, minced
3 heaping tablespoons lard or vegetable oil	2 cups boiling water
½ cup minced celery	½ cup heated oyster juice
½ cup minced onion	Salt and pepper to taste
1 small sweet green pepper, minced	1 pint oysters

Put the rice into the hot lard in a heavy saucepan. Stir until lightly brown and add the celery, onion, green pepper, and garlic. Sauté for about 1 minute; then add the boiling water, oyster juice, and salt and pepper and mix thoroughly. Lower the heat to a simmer, cover, and cook for about 15 minutes, or until the rice is tender. Add the oysters and stir once. Cook for 3 to 5 minutes. If desired, after the rice is cooked, place about 4 pats of butter on top, cover, and allow the butter to melt. Serve as a main course.
Makes 2 to 4 servings.

★

It's been said that there are two types of food at which New Englanders excell—baked goods and ice cream. But with places like the Down-East Village in Yarmouth, Maine, I definitely have to add seafood to that list. Try, for example, this tasty seafood au gratin.

☆ Seafood au Gratin ☆

1 cup (2 sticks) butter	12 ounces fresh crab meat, picked over
1 cup all-purpose flour	8 ounces scallops
½ teaspoon salt	8 ounces Maine shrimp (small shrimp), fresh or frozen, shelled and deveined
½ teaspoon white pepper	
2 cups milk	
12 ounces extra sharp Cheddar cheese, grated	Pinch of paprika
½ cup dry sherry	

Preheat the oven to 400 degrees. In the top of a double boiler over simmering water, melt the butter. Stir in the flour, salt, and pepper. Cook, stirring, for 15 minutes. Whisk in the milk and then the cheese. Cook, stirring occasionally, until thick and smooth. The sauce should be thick enough for a whisk to "stand" in the middle of the pan. Whisk in the sherry.

Place half of the sauce in the bottom of a 9-inch-square baking dish. Distribute all the seafood on top of the sauce. Then cover the seafood with the remaining sauce. Sprinkle with paprika and bake for 20 to 30 minutes, or until bubbly throughout.
Makes 6 to 8 servings.

(Continued)

VARIATION: You can use more fresh Maine crab meat in place of the shrimp for "Maine Crab au Gratin." It's a Down-East tradition and favorite.

★

The Mucky Duck Restaurant on Captiva Island off the Gulf coast of Florida sits right on an expansive white, sandy beach. This place is so popular that unless you get there before 5 P.M. on many days, you'll find you have to park far down the street and you'll likely have to wait an hour, or even two hours, to be seated. But believe me, it's worth it! In fact, many people *enjoy* the wait, as they sit on one of the benches or a rock overlooking the Gulf. It's a pleasure to loll around there, with a big cold pitcher of some drink, watching a beautiful sunset as the sun sinks into the West.

One of the most popular dishes at the Mucky Duck is the Flounder Meunière, which I've found can also be made with egg whites as well as whole eggs, for those who are particularly concerned about cholesterol.

☆ Flounder Meunière ☆

1½ cups dry white wine
Juice of 2 lemons
¼ cup Worcestershire sauce
2 cups all-purpose flour, sifted
White pepper, salt, and paprika
    to taste

6 large eggs
½ handful chopped parsley
8 2- to 4-ounce fresh flounder or
    sole fillets
Butter
Lemon wedges for garnish

Mix together white wine, lemon juice, and Worcestershire sauce in a medium-size mixing bowl.

In a separate dish large enough to flour the fish in, mix together the flour, white pepper, salt, and paprika.

In another medium-size bowl, beat the eggs together with the parsley.

Soak fish fillets in the white wine mixture for 1½ to 2 minutes. Then place the fish in the flour and seasonings and cover completely but lightly. Next, place the fish in the eggs and parsley mixture.

Melt some butter in a frying pan. When the butter is just about to start bubbling, add the fish. Cook for about 2 minutes on each side, or until golden brown. Serve garnished with lemon wedges.
Makes 4 servings.

★

The Captiva Inn on Captiva Island is actually located in the home of Jeannine and George Sterckx. They only take a few dozen couples per night, and they're booked up weeks in advance during the high season. But what you get is well worth the wait: a fabulous seven-course gourmet's delight at a set price.

George and Jeannine, a Belgian couple, moved to Captiva Island from California for the purpose of going into "semi-retirement," as they put it. In 1980, to keep a little cash flow going, they opened a small dining room in their home with four tables. But reality quickly began to outrun their expectations. Their dinners became so popular that four weeks after their opening they had to take the furniture out of their house and convert the whole thing into a larger dining room with a seating capacity of forty.

The atmosphere is not that of a restaurant. It's really a family dining room; and that's exactly the way that George and Jeannine want the Captiva Inn to be known.

Now, try this special shrimp dish from their "home kitchen."

☆ Captiva Inn Shrimp Boat Coquille ☆

2½ cups dry white wine
1 pound small shrimp, shelled
  and deveined
¼ cup (½ stick) butter
2 tablespoons all-purpose flour
1 tablespoon tomato paste (Or
  substitute lobster stock: Boil
  the lobster shells with onion,
  celery, salt, pepper and 1 cup
  lobster meat.)

Salt and pepper to taste
¼ cup heavy cream
½ teaspoon freshly grated
  nutmeg
1 tablespoon lemon juice
6 frozen patty shells, baked

Bring the wine to a boil. Carefully place the shrimp in the wine and simmer very gently for 10 minutes. Remove the shrimp with a slotted spoon and reserve 2 cups of the liquid.

In a separate pan, make a roux with the butter and flour. Gradually add the reserved liquid and cook until slightly thickened. Stir in tomato paste or your reduction of lobster stock and season with salt and pepper. Add the cream, nutmeg, lemon juice, and shrimp. Cook until the

The pose that inspired The Bubble Room's Tropical Snapper à la Carmen Miranda. (Photo courtesy of Hal Bender/National Broadcasting Company, Inc.)

shrimp are heated through. Spoon the shrimp and sauce into the prepared pastry shells. Serve at once.
Makes 6 appetizer servings.

★

The Bubble Room on Captiva Island is a total sensory experience. If you go in at Christmastime, for example, you're likely to find some special scene set up, such as toy elves working in Santa's workshop. Then, when you sit down to eat, you'll find a toy train running around a track built close to the ceiling of the dining room. If your eyes are not drawn to that, you'll be entranced by all the pop memorabilia and photographs from the thirties, forties, and fifties, including candid shots of Dwight Eisenhower and other mid-twentieth-century luminaries, old-fashioned toy airplanes, comic books, and baseball cards.

But the most amazing thing about the Bubble Room is the quantity of fine food they offer. There's probably no restaurant mentioned in this book that will give you more for your money, in terms of *amount* of food, than the Bubble Room.

Their "Snapper à la Carmen Miranda" is a special delicacy concocted just for my benefit, in honor of the Carmen Miranda dress-up routine I did on the *Today Show* a while back.

☆ The Bubble Room's Tropical Snapper ☆ à la Carmen Miranda

4 8- to 9-ounce fresh red snapper fillets	½ cup sugar
2 large eggs	4 firm ripe bananas, peeled and cut lengthwise into a total of 8 halves
1 cup half-and-half	
Salt and pepper to taste	1 cup (2 sticks) butter
2 cups corn flake cereal, ground in a blender to the size of bread crumbs	3 limes, cut into quarters

Wash the snapper fillets in cold water; then pat them dry with paper towels.

Gently beat eggs, half-and-half, salt, and pepper in a mixing bowl. Set aside. *(Continued)*

Put the corn flake crumbs on a plate. Pour the sugar onto a separate plate.

Dip the fillets into the egg mixture and dredge in the corn flakes until fully coated.

Dip the banana halves into egg wash and dredge in the granulated sugar until fully coated.

Melt the butter in a cast-iron skillet and, when it is hot enough to sauté, gently place the snapper fillets on one side of the skillet and the banana halves on the other side. Sauté until golden brown; then turn gently and brown on the second side. The bananas will be ready when the fish is cooked.

Drain and place on a serving platter. Garnish with the lime quarters. Serve with a garden salad tossed with a dressing of mayonnaise blended with lemon juice, garlic, salt, and pepper; rice with turtle peas or black beans; and crispy hot french bread.
Makes 4 servings.

★

As far as I'm concerned, catfish is the unsung hero of American seafood. If I go down for anything in history, I would like to be known as the person who convinced the American people that catfish is one of the finest eating fishes in the world.

Catfish, of course, has developed a bad reputation in some quarters because it's a scavenger. But believe me, if you called it "pisces felinus" and served it with some sort of chichi sauce on a Wedgewood plate—and the waiter who put it in front of you was wearing a tuxedo with gloves—anyone would kill to get the next helping!

Nick's Fishmarket in Chicago was the first "white tablecloth" restaurant in Chicago to serve and popularize catfish. In fact, the restaurant's seafood supplier says that Nick's has singlehandedly turned this item into one of the city's biggest selling fish.

So I had to include Nick's catfish specialties among the recipes below. Also, you'll find mahi mahi from Hawaiian waters, abalone, and a variety of other seafood specialties, with Nick's special recipe touch.

☆ Catfish Fishmarket Style (Lemon-Butter Sauce) ☆

2 pounds catfish fillets
All-purpose flour

2 large eggs, beaten
¾ cup vegetable oil

SAUCE
6 tablespoons butter
1 tablespoon chopped parsley

Juice of 2 lemons

Dust the fillets with the flour and then dip them into the eggs. Heat vegetable oil in a large frying pan until it is very hot. Add the fish and sauté until golden on both sides, 7 to 10 minutes total. Remove to a heated platter and keep warm.

To make the sauce, melt the butter in a saucepan. Add the parsley and lemon juice to taste. Spoon the lemon-butter sauce over the fillets and garnish with additional parsley, if desired.
Makes 6 servings.

☆ Swordfish Stavros ☆

1 10-ounce bag spinach
4 ounces feta cheese
4 ounces fresh dill, finely
  chopped
1 medium-size onion, diced
1 chicken bouillon cube

¼ teaspoon ground nutmeg
¼ teaspoon salt
¼ teaspoon white pepper
2 teaspoons dried oregano
1 cup olive oil
8 4- to 8-ounce swordfish steaks

Wash and dry spinach; then chop it fine. Mix the feta cheese and dill in a bowl with the spinach.

In a large skillet, sauté the onion, chicken base, nutmeg, salt, pepper, and oregano with the olive oil. Cook until the onion is translucent. Remove from the heat and let cool slightly; then add the onion mixture to the spinach. Top each grilled swordfish steak with an ample portion of the spinach mixture.
Makes 8 servings.

Note: Any unused sauce can be refrigerated, covered, for about 1 week.

☆ Mahi Mahi Chicago Style ☆

DEMI-GLACE
2 beef bouillon cubes
2½ cups boiling water
2 sprigs parsley
¼ cup (½ stick) butter
6 tablespoons all-purpose flour

SAUCE
1 teaspoon olive oil
1 large onion, diced
4 ounces mushrooms, diced

2 tomatoes, peeled and diced
½ teaspoon dried thyme
Pinch of white pepper
2 tablespoons dry white wine
½ cup demi-glace (from recipe
  left)
½ large zucchini, cut into
  julienne

SEAFOOD
8 4-ounce mahi mahi fillets
¾ cup vegetable oil

To prepare the demi-glace, dissolve the bouillon cubes in the boiling water. Add the parsley and simmer for 10 minutes. Remove the parsley and return to a boil.

In a separate pan, melt the butter; then stir in the flour to make a thick paste. Add the paste to the boiling bouillon and stir until the glace reaches a medium consistency.

To prepare the sauce, heat the olive oil in a frying pan; then add the onion and sauté until it is brown. Add the mushrooms and tomatoes and sauté for 2 minutes, or just until hot. Add the seasonings and white wine. Then combine the sauce with the demi-glace and add zucchini.

To prepare the fish, sauté the mahi mahi fillets for 4 minutes on each side in the oil heated to 350 degrees. Put 2 fillets on each plate and top with the sauce. Serve at once.
Makes 4 servings.

☆ Fishmarket Catfish with Dill Sauce ☆

CATFISH
2 pounds catfish fillets
2 large eggs, beaten
¾ cup vegetable oil
All-purpose flour

DILL SAUCE
¼ cup (½ stick) butter
1 tablespoon lemon juice
½ teaspoon chopped dill
¼ cup demi-glace

DEMI-GLACE
2 beef bouillon cubes
2½ cups boiling water
2 sprigs parsley
¼ cup (½ stick) butter
6 tablespoons all-purpose flour

GARNISH
Lemon wedges
Parsley sprigs

To prepare the catfish, dust the fillets with flour and dip them into the eggs. Heat the oil until very hot in a frying pan. Add the fish and sauté until golden on both sides (7 to 10 minutes). Remove to a heated platter and warm.

Meanwhile, prepare the demi-glace: Dissolve the bouillon cubes in the boiling water. Add the parsley and simmer for 10 minutes. Remove the parsley and return to a boil.

In a separate pan, melt the butter and stir in the flour to make a thick paste. Add the paste to the boiling bouillon and stir until glace has reached a medium consistency. (Refrigerate extra demi-glace and serve, after reheating, as a garnish with other seafoods.)

To prepare the dill sauce, heat the butter and lemon juice in a small saucepan. Add the dill and demi-glace. Cook and stir until heated through and blended.

Spoon the dill sauce over the fillets and garnish with lemon wedges and parsley.

Makes 4 to 6 servings.

☆　Casino Butter and Shellfish　☆

CASINO BUTTER
1 cup (2 sticks) butter, softened
½ bunch parsley sprigs, finely
　chopped
1 tablespoon brandy
1 tablespoon dry white wine
2 dashes of Tabasco sauce
2 dashes of Angostura bitters
2 dashes of Worcestershire sauce
2 garlic cloves, finely chopped

¼ cup diced pimiento
1 small sweet green pepper,
　diced

SHELLFISH
2 dozen clams or oysters
Parmesan cheese
Bacon Strips

GARNISH
Lemon wedges
Parsley sprigs

(Continued)

To make the Casino butter, combine all ingredients in a bowl, stirring constantly or blending with an electric mixer. When combined, place the mixture on a piece of aluminum foil and mold it into a 1-inch-diameter log shape. Then refrigerate or freeze it.

To prepare the shellfish, preheat the oven to 450 degrees. Clean and scrub the clams or oysters. On each open bivalve, sprinkle some Parmesan cheese and a pat of Casino Butter sliced from the log. Top with a small uncooked square of bacon. Bake for 9 to 10 minutes. Garnish with lemon wedges and parsley.
Makes 3 to 4 servings.

☆ Abalone Ricci ☆

4 5-ounce fresh abalone fillets	1 teaspoon chopped fresh dill
All-purpose flour	3 ounces bay shrimp
4 large eggs, beaten	10 medium-size mushrooms,
Vegetable oil	sliced
¼ cup (½ stick) butter	8 asparagus spears, steamed and
½ teaspoon lemon juice	chopped
	Parsley sprigs for garnish

Pound abalone fillets to tenderize them. Dust both sides of each piece in flour; then dip both sides of each fillet in the beaten eggs. Heat ¼ inch of oil in a large frying pan. Brown fillets over high heat, turning once. (The total cooking time should be about 1 minute.)

To make the sauce, melt the butter in frying pan. Add the lemon juice and dill. Cook for 1 minute. Add bay shrimp, mushrooms, and asparagus. Cook over medium heat for 2 to 3 minutes, or until all the ingredients are heated through. Spoon the sauce over the abalone and garnish with parsley.
Makes 4 servings.

★

I mentioned earlier something about regional philosophies of barbecue. As I said, in many parts of the Deep South, barbecue is synonymous with pork—you can't have barbecue with beef or any other type of meat.

But America, of course, is the melting pot and we've found ways to combine barbecue sauces with all sorts of things. In this recipe, you have a barbecue connected with a pork dish—bacon—but then, completely out of left field, the Mucky Duck Restaurant in Captiva Island suggests that you throw in some shrimp. And I must say, the result is absolutely incredible, and tasty enough to satisfy any barbecue purist!

☆ Barbecue Shrimp Wrapped with Bacon ☆

PER PERSON
1 12-inch metal skewer
5 large shrimp, shelled but with
    tails left on
2½ slices bacon (half a slice for
    each shrimp)

OUR SAUCE
1 16-ounce jar Cattleman's Bar-
    B-Que Sauce or substitute
    your favorite

6 tablespoons Worcestershire
    sauce
6 tablespoons bottled
    horseradish (you might like
    less or more)

EQUIPMENT
Outdoor barbecue grill
Cooking tongs
Brush to spread sauce as shrimp
    cook

When wrapping the shrimp with the bacon, you start at the top of the tail and wrap tightly to the bottom of the shrimp. Push the skewer through each shrimp starting at the top, through the slice of bacon, down to the bottom of the shrimp, and through the bacon a second time. Each skewer should hold 5 shrimp.

Place the filled skewers on the grill over a medium flame. Combine sauce ingredients, and brush the shrimp with the sauce as they cook, turning and brushing often. Cook until the shrimp are bright pink and the bacon is crisp.

★

There are dozens of ways to prepare that king of the sea crawlers, the lobster. But one of my favorites is a refreshing lobster salad, with all sorts of vegetables and other things mixed artfully in. I have yet to find anyone who does this dish any closer to perfection than Le Pèrigord Park in Manhattan.

☆ Lobster Salad ☆

2 3-pound lobsters, boiled
½ cup Cognac
2 whole black truffles
4 fresh mushrooms

Salt and pepper to taste
1 head Boston lettuce
1 celery stalk or shallot
2 artichoke bottoms
½ cup fine olive oil
Pinch each of thyme, chopped
    parsley, and chervil

Discard the shells of the lobsters and cut the meat into big chunks (use the claws also). Macerate in a good Cognac with the truffles and mushrooms. Season with salt and pepper.

In another bowl, cut the head of lettuce into very thin shreds (this is called a chiffonade). Also slice the celery and artichoke bottoms into julienne, and add the olive oil. At the last minute, before serving, add the macerated lobster; mix and sprinkle with thyme, parsley, and chervil.

Makes 2 to 4 servings.

★

Some people get turned off by the idea of eating snails; I suppose that's why most top-flight restaurants call them by the fancy French name, "escargot." I may have felt that way myself at one point, but I've loved escargot for so long that I honestly can't remember ever *not* liking it.

Of course, it's got to be prepared just right, and that's where the Colonial Williamsburg kitchen comes forward to help us with this recipe.

☆ Escargots Regency ☆

4 shallots, minced
1 garlic clove, minced
2 teaspoons butter
24 escargots

Pinch of saffron threads
2 teaspoons Pernod
4 ounces spinach, washed and
    drained

Sauté half the minced shallots and half the garlic in one teaspoon butter. Add the drained escargots and sauté well over high heat. Stir in the saffron. Add the Pernod and ignite with a long kitchen match.

In a separate pan, melt the remaining butter and add the remaining garlic and shallots. Sauté quickly. Then add the spinach and sauté for a few minutes more. Put the spinach on the bottom of an oven proof dish. Arrange the escargots on top and nap the ends of the escargots with Glaçage. Brown quickly in a very hot oven. Serve with garlic bread. *Makes 4 servings.*

☆ Glaçage ☆

Make the basic hollandaise sauce as follows.

5 teaspoons white vinegar	3 large egg yolks, beaten
1 tablespoon chopped shallots	¼ cup heavy cream
2 to 3 black peppercorns, crushed	1½ cups clarified butter
	Juice of half a lemon
5 teaspoons water	Salt and pepper

In a small saucepan reduce vinegar, shallots, and peppercorns.

Add water and egg yolks. Stir into a fairly thick cream over simmering water. Now slowly add the clarified butter. When all the butter is incorporated, season with lemon juice, salt, and pepper. Beat the heavy cream until it's very stiff, and fold into hollandaise sauce.

★

Wintzell's Oyster House in Mobile, Alabama, is just a straight sail over the Gulf of Mexico from the West Indies. In other words, there's a direct link with some of those fantastic seafood dishes from the Caribbean islands, of which this West Indies Salad is a prime example.

☆ West Indies Salad ☆

4 large onions, diced	2 cups cider vinegar
4 pounds fresh lump crab meat	1 cup vegetable oil
4 tablespoons salt	2 cups ice and water
2 tablespoons pepper	

(Continued)

Layer the ingredients in a large container in the following order: one third of the onions, 2 pounds of the crab meat, one third of the onions, 2 tablespoons of the salt, 1 tablespoon of the pepper, 2 pounds of the crab meat, one third of the onions, 2 tablespoons of the salt, 1 tablespoon of the pepper, the vinegar, the oil, and the ice and water.

Cover and refrigerate for at least 8 hours. Mix thoroughly before serving.
Makes 6 to 8 servings.

★

There's nothing in the world quite like Joe's Stone Crab Restaurant in Miami Beach, Florida. They select the best stone crabs to be found anywhere in the world, and the daily standing-room-only crowds testify to the restaurant staff's ability to put together a superior seafood menu.

There are a lot of great things that Joe's has to offer besides the crabs: outstanding New England Clam Chowder and Key Lime Pie. But perhaps the thing that really pushes Joe's over the top is the special mustard sauce they serve with the crabs.

Mustard sauce is a tasty item with any food, but as far as I'm concerned, it was *made* for stone crabs. Even as you wait to get into Joe's, you find yourself consistently in one of the happiest lines of customers you'll ever see in your life. And I have to believe this exuberance arises largely from the anticipation of that fantastic mustard sauce. Here's the secret recipe, a gift directly from Joe's Stone Crab Restaurant to you.

☆ Mustard Sauce ☆

1 tablespoon dry mustard	1 teaspoon A-1 Sauce
1 cup mayonnaise	1¼ tablespoons light cream
2 teaspoons Worcestershire sauce	⅛ teaspoon salt

Beat all the ingredients together for about 3 minutes. Cover and chill before serving.

★

Chadwick's Restaurant, on the South Seas Plantation Resort acreage on Captiva Island, Florida, makes some of the finest seafood dishes I've ever tasted. Here are two of the top specialties from their fine kitchen.

All the treasures of the sea can be found at Chadwick's Restaurant on Captiva Island, Florida. (Photo © 1986 Clement Photographic Services)

☆ Seafood Boca Grande ☆

6 large shrimp
6 sea scallops
2 tablespoons chopped clams
6 tablespoons diced grouper
¼ cup sliced mushrooms
1 tablespoon chopped scallions
¼ cup (½ stick) butter
1 tablespoon dry white wine

1 tablespoon lime juice
1 garlic clove, chopped
1 tablespoon chopped shallots
6 tablespoons heavy cream
4 tablespoons grated Parmesan
  cheese
Salt and pepper to taste
8 ounces fettuccini, cooked
Chopped parsley

Sauté the seafood, mushrooms, and scallions in the butter until the shrimp are pink and the vegetables are tender.

Add the wine, lime juice, garlic, and shallots and reduce the liquid by one third.

(Continued)

89

Add the cream and reduce the liquid by half. Stir in the Parmesan cheese and season with salt and pepper. Serve over a bed of hot fettuccini; sprinkle with chopped parsley and additional Parmesan cheese. *Makes 1 serving.*

☆ Snapper Tortuga ☆

8 ounces snapper fillet	2 tablespoons white wine
Pinch each of dried basil and oregano	¼ cup (½ stick) butter
1 tablespoon lime juice	¼ cup sliced mushrooms
Salt and pepper to taste	2 tablespoons chopped scallions
3 ½-inch slices of tomato	1 tablespoon dry sherry
4 tablespoons grated Parmesan cheese	6 tablespoons heavy cream
	1 ounce baby shrimp
	Chopped parsley

Preheat the oven to 350 degrees. Rub snapper with herbs and lime juice and seasonings. Top with the sliced tomatoes and half of the cheese and place in a baking dish. Pour in the wine and dot with half the butter. Bake until tender and soft to the touch, about 15 minutes.

In a frying pan, melt the remaining butter and sauté mushrooms and scallions. Add the sherry and ignite it. Add the cream, lower the heat, and simmer until thick. Stir in the remaining cheese.

Transfer the snapper to a dish and pour the sauce over it. Garnish with the baby shrimp and a sprinkle of chopped parsley.
Makes 1 serving.

★

The most incredible crab meat roll I've ever had in my life comes from The Pioneer Club in Lake Charles, Louisiana. But you don't have to go to the bayou country to enjoy it. Here's the original recipe for you to try in your own kitchen.

☆ Crab Meat Rolls ☆

CRÊPES
1 cup all-purpose flour
1 cup milk
1 large egg
3 tablespoons vegetable oil

CREAM SAUCE
1¼ cups all-purpose flour
½ cup (1 stick) butter, melted
2 quarts milk
8 drops yellow food coloring
Salt and white pepper to taste

CRAB MEAT MIXTURE
½ sweet green pepper, chopped
    fine
½ white onion, chopped fine
1 tablespoon butter
1 pound lump crab meat

Grated Cheddar cheese
Lemon wedges

To make the crêpes, mix all the ingredients together in a bowl. Pour a small amount into a hot 6-inch skillet. When golden on one side, flip over and cook on the other side. Continue until all the mixture has been used.

To make the sauce, mix flour and melted butter together in a large saucepan; then add the remaining ingredients, stirring constantly. Continue cooking until the liquid is reduced, and the mixture is a thick sauce consistency. This sauce should cool down before being poured on the crêpes.

To make the crab meat mixture, sauté the vegetables in the butter until tender. Add the crab meat and ½ cup of the cream sauce mixture and mix. Remove from the heat.

Put about ¼ cup of this mixture into a crêpe and roll. Continue this process until all of the crab meat mixture has been used. Put one or two crêpes on an ovenproof plate. Take a large mixing spoon and evenly cover the crêpes with the cream sauce mixture. Cover this with grated Cheddar cheese. Bake in a 400-degree oven for 10 to 12 minutes. The cheese should be completely melted and bubbly. Garnish with lemon wedges. Serve immediately.
Makes 2 to 4 servings.

☆ 4 ☆

Country Specials

I'm definitely a country boy at heart.

Sure, I work in the city, and I spend many of my off-hours in urban areas. But I know that the essence of Willard Scott lies on my Virginia farm, where I try to spend all my weekends with my family. So it's natural that the kind of meals that would appeal to me most is what might be called, in the broadest sense, "country cooking."

I don't by any means limit the idea of "country" cuisine to any one part of the country or, for that matter, to any specific ethnic or national tradition. I guess that for me, real country cooking has to have an American flavor or twist of some sort. But beyond that, my own personal tastes and definitions of what constitutes a "country special" are virtually without limit. In this part of the book, then, I want to focus on the finest homey but exquisite dishes, which for the most part involve fowl, pork, and on-the-hoof meats.

Country cooking is often characterized by quantity as well as quality. So what better place to begin than with a steak specialty from the Bubble Room on Captiva Island, which combines the best of quality and quantity.

☆ **Rouladen of Flanken Florentine** ☆

---

1 large flank steak (about 2 to
  2½ pounds)
1 garlic clove, minced
1 8-ounce package cream
  cheese, softened

½ cup drained and chopped
  pimiento
1 cup thinly sliced mushrooms
1 cup whole fresh spinach
  leaves, drained and cooked

4 to 5 ounces thinly sliced
  Parma ham
16 to 20 whole peeled baby
  onions (1 to 1½ inches in
  diameter)

2 cups beef broth
2 cups medium-dry or dry red
  wine
1 or 2 bay leaves
Salt and coarsely ground pepper

Preheat the oven to 350 degrees. To butterfly the flanken, lay the steak flat on the counter with the length away from you. Using a long fillet knife, slide the blade horizontally through the side until it almost reaches the opposite side. Carefully split the meat in half by slowly working the knife away from you. Spread the meat open.

Rub the meat with the garlic. Then spread cream cheese over the entire surface of the meat. Sprinkle the pimientos over the cheese; then sprinkle the mushrooms over the pimientos. Lay the spinach leaves over the entire surface (2 to 3 leaves thick). Lay ham slices over the spinach.

Carefully roll the meat beginning with the narrow end. Continue rolling and secure the end with toothpicks. Then put the rouladen into a 9- by 12-inch roasting pan.

Surround the meat roll with the onions. Pour broth and wine over the meat and submerge the bay leaves into the broth. Bake for 1 hour.

Drain cooked broth from the meat and onions, reserving the liquid for gravy. Set the meat and onions aside and keep warm. Thicken the broth into a thin gravy, adding salt and pepper to taste.

To serve, slice the rouladen into thin slices. Ladle the gravy over the meat and serve the onions on the side.
Makes 4 servings.

★

The Gourmet House in Bismarck, North Dakota, is truly an all-American establishment. We've already seen what they can do with a pecan pie and a salad dish—but consider this fantastic way of cooking a steak, South American style. It's truly a consummate combination of the tastiest North Dakota beef and the tangiest Latin style of cooking.

☆ South American Steak ☆

1 20-ounce bottle Kikkoman soy
   sauce
1 10-ounce bottle
   Worcestershire sauce
1 10-ounce bottle steak sauce
2 5-ounce bottles Heinz 57
   Sauce
1 pound packed dark brown
   sugar
2 teaspoons Tabasco sauce

2 teaspoons garlic powder
2 teaspoons onion powder
1 teaspoon black pepper
1 teaspoon celery salt
1 teaspoon lemon juice
⅓ cup prepared mustard
24 12- to 14-ounce rib, rib eye,
   or chuck steak

Mix all the ingredients *except* the steak together in a large glass or stainless steel bowl. The ingredients in their raw state might well eat the enamel off your bathtub: It would almost certainly evaporate a plastic bowl! Makes 2 quarts. Store any unused sauce covered in the refrigerator. It should keep for several weeks.

To use, simply brush one side of the steak in the sauce. Broil in an oven broiler, sauce side up, or pan-broil in a cast-iron skillet, sauce side down. When you turn the steak, brush the other side in the sauce and finish cooking. (Note: Don't place a used steak brush back into any unused sauce, or the sauce may go sour.)

Brush on a bit more sauce and serve. For variety, add your favorite liquor—bourbon, brandy, gin—to the sauce.
Makes 24 single-steak servings.

★

Now, for good old standard American fare, try this Roast Prime Rib of Beef preparation from the Wayside Inn, in Middletown, Virginia.

☆ Roast Prime Rib of Beef ☆

1 18- to 20-pound standing rib
   roast

Salt, pepper, rosemary, and
   garlic powder to taste

Preheat the oven to 350 degrees. Place the whole rib roast, bones down, in an uncovered roasting pan. Sprinkle generously with the sea-

94

sonings. Slice through the layer of fat down to the meat portion forming a flap. Lift the flap of fat and season the meat. Put the flap back and roast the meat for approximately 2½ hours for rare to medium-rare. Serve au jus with a popover, if desired.
Makes 6 to 8 servings.

★

For a real outdoorsy, almost camp-out feeling when you're sitting down at your dinner table, try these two dishes from West Virginia's famous Greenbrier Restaurant—smoked sirloin and smoked duck marinade.

☆ Smoked Sirloin ☆

2 cups olive oil
¼ cup brown mustard
2 tablespoons salt
½ cup balsamic vinegar
¼ cup sugar

1 teaspoon cracked black pepper
2 garlic cloves, chopped
1 teaspoon Worcestershire sauce
1 teaspoon lemon juice
1 pound sirloin strip steak

Combine all the ingredients *except* the steak in a large plastic bag. Add the steak and marinate overnight. Hot smoke to the desired doneness. Use any leftover marinade on chicken, chops, etc.
Makes 2 to 3 servings.

☆ Duck Marinade ☆

1 gallon water
1 pound kosher salt
2 tablespoons curing salt (see Glossary)
2 tablespoons sugar

½ cup honey
1 cup Madeira wine
Bouquet garnie (see Glossary)
1 3½- to 4-pound duckling

Combine all ingredients in a large bowl, cover, and marinate overnight. Cold smoke for 4 to 6 hours. Hot smoke until cooked.
Makes 2 servings.

★

Sometimes I wonder if we've lost our creative edge in the kitchen these days, especially when I consider how they're able to recapture Colonial creativity at the Colonial Williamsburg in Virginia. They just took a close look at all the fabulous foods that they had available and then sat down and came up with interesting ways to put them together.

Here, those early colonists took chicken breasts, crab meat, apples, and a variety of other tasty ingredients, to produce this Chicken Chesapeake, which Colonial Williamsburg has fortunately preserved for our enjoyment.

☆ Chicken Chesapeake ☆

1 tablespoon butter
6 shallots, minced
2 apples, diced
Salt and pepper to taste
1 cup apple brandy
1 pound crab meat, picked over

4 8-ounce boneless whole
    chicken breasts
All-purpose flour
4 large egg whites
2 large egg yolks

Melt the butter in a pan. Add the shallots and apples and season with salt and pepper to taste. When the butter is foamy, add the apple brandy. Cook until the mixture is dry. Transfer to a bowl and add the crab meat. Preheat the oven to 325 degrees.

Pound chicken breasts flat. Season with a little salt and pepper. Divide the crab meat and apple mixture into quarters. Spread a portion on each chicken breast. Fold the breasts in half to enclose the filling and hold them closed with toothpicks. Roll the breasts in flour and dip them in a mixture of the beaten egg whites and egg yolks.

Put the breasts in a lightly greased pan and bake for 20 to 30 minutes. *Makes 4 servings.*

★

Now, get ready for some real wild, frontier cooking! You may actually have to do some hunting (in the woods, not the supermarket!) for some of these foods. The rabbit, for example, will be available in some meat stores, but not in all.

At first glance, some of the combinations may seem a litte crazy: For example, roast turkey with peanut dressing? I can already hear some of the comments: "Come on, Willard, let's get serious!"

But let me remind you again: The early Americans were often much more creative than we are when they developed their absolutely unforgettable recipes. I expect the following recipes, all from the Wayside Inn in Middletown, Virginia, will have a similar impact on you.

☆ Wayside's Fried Rabbit ☆

1 2½- to 3 pound rabbit, cut into 6 pieces
¼ teaspoon dried basil
1 onion, peeled
1 large carrot, diced
1 celery stalk, diced
Salt and pepper to taste
Milk and all-purpose flour for coating
Peanut oil for frying

Boil the rabbit with the basil, onion, carrot, and celery in water to cover for approximately 30 minutes, or until it is tender. Remove the rabbit from the cooking liquid and allow it to cool slightly. Bone the rabbit and cut the meat into large pieces. Sprinkle with salt and pepper. Then dip the rabbit first into milk and then into the flour to coat it. Fry in hot peanut oil until golden brown on all sides.

Serve over brown or wild rice and garnish with fried mushrooms and onion rings.
Makes 4 servings.

☆ Wayside Inn Pan-Fried Chicken ☆

½ cup seasoned salt
2 3-pound fryers, halved or quartered
All-purpose flour for coating
Peanut oil or vegetable shortening for frying

Sprinkle the salt over the chicken; then dip the chicken into the flour just before frying. Place in a cast-iron skillet with enough hot oil to cover the chicken. Cook over medium to medium-high heat, turning the chicken until it is golden brown and tender, approximately 40 minutes.
Makes 5 to 6 servings.

☆ Huntsman Pie ☆

1 pound cubed venison	1 quart (4 cups) stock (juices
1 rabbit	from venison and rabbit)
1 pound duck meat	⅔ cup port
¼ cup (½ stick) butter	2 teaspoons Kitchen Bouquet
1 garlic clove, minced	Pearl onions, bacon strips, fried
⅓ cup all-purpose flour	button mushrooms, and
¼ cup grape jelly	parsley sprigs

Roast the duck at 350 degrees for 1 hour, or until tender, remove the bones, and cut the meat into bite-sized pieces. Place the cubed uncooked venison and uncooked rabbit in separate pans, season with salt and pepper, and add water to cover. Simmer until tender, 1½ hours.

Remove the venison and rabbit from the stock and reserve the cooking liquid. Bone the rabbit. Melt the butter and add the garlic. Sauté for 2 minutes. Add the flour and cook for 10 more minutes. Add the reserved stock and grape jelly.

Whip the sauce until smooth and cook for an additional 15 minutes. Add the port and Kitchen Bouquet and season to taste.

Cover each casserole with a pastry crust. Place into the oven at 350 degrees for approximately 20 minutes, or until the crust is golden brown. Remove from the oven and garnish with a pearl onion, a small strip of bacon, and button mushrooms. Place parsley sprig alongside the garnish.
Makes 8 to 10 servings.

☆ Roast Turkey with Peanut Dressing ☆

1 12- to 14-pound turkey	Peanut Dressing (recipe follows)
Salt	Melted butter or vegetable oil

Preheat the oven to 325 degrees. Remove the giblets from the large cavity of the turkey, and remove the neck from the neck cavity; reserve for giblet gravy. Rinse the turkey thoroughly with cold water and pat dry with paper towels. Rub both cavities lightly with salt.

Fill the neck cavity with a small amount of the Peanut Dressing, and fasten skin to the back with a skewer. Lightly stuff the large cavity with the dressing. Fold the wing tips across the back of the turkey; tuck the drumsticks under the band of skin at the tail, or tie them securely to the tail.

Brush the entire bird with melted butter and put on a rack, breast side up, in a roasting pan. Insert a meat thermometer in the thickest part of thigh, making sure it does not touch the bone. Bake until the meat thermometer registers 185 degrees (about 4½ to 5 hours).

If the turkey starts to brown too much, cover it loosely with a tent of aluminum foil. When the turkey is two thirds done, cut band of skin or string holding the drumsticks. The turkey is done when the drumsticks move up and down easily. Let rest for 15 to 20 minutes before carving. Garnish as desired.
Makes 14 to 16 servings.

☆ Peanut Dressing ☆

¾ cup finely chopped onion	2 cups chopped salted peanuts
1½ cups finely chopped celery	1 tablespoon salt
½ cup chopped fresh parsley	1 tablespoon pepper
1 cup (2 sticks) butter, melted	1 tablespoon rubbed sage
12 cups soft bread crumbs	4½ cups water

Sauté the onion, celery, and parsley in the butter in a large Dutch oven until tender. Add the remaining ingredients and mix well. Spoon the dressing into the turkey cavities. Spoon the remaining dressing into a greased baking dish. Bake at 325 degrees for 45 minutes to 1 hour, or until lightly browned around the edges.
Makes 12 servings.

★

The internationally known Louisiana Cajun chef, Paul Prudhomme, has become a good friend; we've eaten together and appeared beside each other on national television.

Reared south of Opelousas, Louisiana, in Acadian country, Chef Paul began cooking with his mother when he was seven years old. The youngest of 13 children, he was heir to a 200-year heritage of French cooking in the area where he grew up.

"With seven or eight kids still at home," he says, "it was like running a small restaurant. We didn't have electricity, so we didn't have refrigeration. We used only what was fresh, in season. I've continued to do

Paul Prudhomme—the man responsible for popularizing Cajun cooking —and Willard. (Photo courtesy of Paul Prudhomme)

this in my career as a chef. I know that fresh ingredients of good quality are the most important factor in preparing exceptional food."

And I say amen to that.

The first time I met Paul Prudhomme was when I was sent down to New Orleans to cover the Mardi Gras for the *Today Show* in 1982. Somebody said, "You ought to go to K-Paul's." So we decided to go, even though there was an incredible line—and this was before his national reputation had completely developed! Cajun cooking was just starting to emerge in those days.

In a sense, it was an instant "love affair." He's big and I'm big, and we really enjoy talking to each other and eating together. Ceratinly, I'm crazy about Chef Paul's cooking, but I'm even crazier about him as a person.

Now, here's one of Chef Paul's specialties, some blackened pork chops, which I'm sure you'll want to try when you're doing some cooking outdoors.

☆ Blackened Pork Chops ☆

This dish may smoke you out of the kitchen, but it's worth it! It's better to cook it outdoors on a gas grill or butane burner. Or you can use a charcoal grill, but only if you add 8 to 10 chunks of hickory or other wood. As the wood burns up, continue to add more pieces of hickory to other wood chunks. (A charcoal fire doesn't get hot enough to "blacken" the chops properly.)

SEASONING MIX (or substitute
   Cajun Magic Pork and Veal
   Magic)
2 tablespoons plus 1½ teaspoons
   salt
2½ teaspoons onion powder
2½ teaspoons ground red pepper
   (preferably cayenne)
2 teaspoons garlic powder
1¼ teaspoons white pepper

1¼ teaspoons dry mustard
1¼ teaspoons rubbed sage
1¼ teaspoons ground cumin
1¼ teaspoons black pepper
1¼ teaspoons dried thyme leaves

18 4- to 5-ounce pork chops
   suitable for broiling, cut ½-
   inch thick

Combine seasoning ingredients, and cover each side of each chop generously and evenly (use between ¼ and ½ teaspoon on each side), patting it in with your hands. (Use the remaining seasoning mix in another pork recipe.)

Let the chops come to room temperature. This should take about 1 hour.

Heat the serving plates in a 250-degree oven.

Heat a large cast-iron skillet over very high heat until it is beyond the smoking stage. You should see white ash in the skillet bottom (the skillet can't be too hot for this dish). This will take at least 10 minutes.

Place the chops in the hot skillet in a single layer. Cook, uncovered, over very high heat for about 1 to 2 minutes, until the underside forms a crust. Turn the chops over and cook until done to your liking.

Repeat with remaining chops (wipe any excess oil from the skillet after cooking each batch). Serve each chop while piping hot, allowing 3 chops per person.

Makes 6 servings.

★

The United States has a reputation for being a melting pot of all peoples, from every nation on earth. So it's natural that our foods would follow suit. In other words, in the "pots" in many kitchens across America, we've put in the best ingredients and used techniques of cooking from many different lands. As a result, we've consistently found our own special, distinctive style of preparing them.

The Beef Stroganoff at Le Pèrigord Park Restaurant in Manhattan is one example of how effectively this transfer of meals from the Old World to the New can take place.

☆ Beef Stroganoff for Four ☆

1 pound fillet of beef
Salt, white pepper, and
   Hungarian paprika to taste
2 onions, sliced
8 to 10 tablespoons butter
1 tablespoon all-purpose flour

½ cup dry white wine
½ cup red wine vinegar
1 cup beef broth
2 tablespoons sour cream
2 tablespoons vegetable oil

Cut the beef into narrow strips, approximately 1 inch long. Season with salt, white pepper, and Hungarian paprika.

Cook the onions in a frying pan in the butter for 10 minutes. Add the flour and ½ teaspoon of paprika and stir until the mixture is smooth. Deglaze the pan with the white wine, vinegar, and beef broth. Let the sauce reduce until it has reached the desired consistency. Then add the sour cream and cook for another 10 minutes. Pass the sauce through a very fine strainer into a clean pan. Keep it warm.

Heat the oil and, when it is very hot, brown the meat on both sides. Drain the meat and add the sauce. Serve very hot.

★

Venison, the meat of a deer, is often characterized as having a "strong taste." Yet many people find it to be one of the finest-tasting meats around.

At Vienna '79 in New York City, they've developed a quintessential venison recipe, which I've included below. But before you get into your actual cooking, you might be interested in this little piece of history which the restaurant has shared with me.

Game dishes have been an integral part of Austrian cooking since the Middle Ages. Originally, game could only be enjoyed by the land-owning aristocracy, which long retained the sole privilege of hunting. (Sounds like Robin Hood's problems with killing the king's deer, doesn't it?)

By the nineteenth century, however, hunting deer had become open to everyone, and game recipes even got included in cookbooks used by the middle class. By the 1880s, the "Wildbretmarkt," the game market in Vienna, was celebrated for the variety of delicacies gathered from the entire empire.

Today, hunting—and feasting on the results of the hunt—is still popular in Austria, and Vienna '79 continues this Austrian tradition.

☆ Sautéed Venison Fillets and Red Currant Sauce ☆

5 tablespoons oil for frying
6 whole 5- to 6-ounce venison
    fillets (tenderloin of venison),
    trimmed of fat and sprinkled
    with salt and pepper
4 tablespoons red currants

2 tablespoons sugar
1 teaspoon sherry vinegar
¾ cup game stock (see note)
2 tablespoons butter
Salt and white pepper to taste

(Continued)

Heat some oil in a frying pan and sauté the venison fillets for about 3 minutes on each side. They should be brown outside and pink inside. Remove and keep warm in a covered plate.

Add 3 tablespoons of currants, sugar, and sherry vinegar to the pan and sauté briefly. Add the game stock and bring to a boil; cool to reduce by half. Strain the sauce into a clean pan and then swirl in the butter. Season with salt and pepper and keep warm over low heat.

To serve, carve the venison fillets against the grain into long slices. Pour the currant sauce on warm plates and arrange the venison slices in a circular pattern on the sauce. Sprinkle with the remaining currants and serve at once.
Makes 6 servings.

Note: Regular brown sauce is fine for game stock. The chef suggests making stock from bones: Use standard brown beef stock recipe, substituting venison ingredients for beef.

★

Now, for a little Latin American flavor, try this Chicken Marengo from The Wigwam in Litchfield Park, Arizona.

☆ Chicken Marengo ☆

1 large onion, thinly sliced	1 cup dry white wine
2 garlic cloves, crushed	½ cup brown veal sauce
½ cup olive oil	1½ cups button mushrooms, washed
2 to 3 2½-pound frying chickens, quartered	2 cups pearl onions, blanched and peeled
Salt and pepper	¼ cup clarified butter or olive oil
½ teaspoon dried thyme	
2 bay leaves	½ cup sliced pitted green olives
1½ cups chicken stock or broth	½ cup sliced pitted black olives
2 cups Italian tomatoes, crushed by hand	2 tablespoons chopped parsley

In a large frying pan, sauté the onion and crushed garlic briefly in the oil. Remove and set aside.

Sprinkle the chicken with salt and pepper and brown it on all sides in the pan. Remove the chicken and set it aside. Add the thyme, bay leaves, chicken stock, tomatoes, wine, and veal sauce. Mix well. Return the chicken and sautéed onion and garlic and bring to a boil. Cover and simmer until the chicken is tender, about 20 to 25 minutes. Turn the chicken once after about 15 minutes.

Remove the chicken and keep it warm. Reduce the sauce for 15 to 20 minutes over medium heat; then strain the sauce. Season with salt and pepper, if necessary.

Meanwhile, in a frying pan, sauté the mushrooms and blanched onions in the butter until golden brown. Serve the chicken garnished with the mushrooms, pearl onions, green and black olives, and parsley.
Makes 6 to 8 servings.

★

The Tee Pee Mexican Food Restaurant in Phoenix, Arizona, is owned and operated by Tony and Anna Duran. This family-owned establishment is one of the most popular restaurants in the Phoenix area, and I always try to go there when I'm in the vicinity. The place has had only two cooks since it was founded in 1960, and continuity in the kitchen has certainly contributed to making the Durans' place reach the apex of Mexican food.

As an example of what I'm talking about, try these Chiles Relleno.

☆ Chiles Relleno ☆

4 eggs, separated
½ cup shredded Wisconsin
yellow Cheddar cheese

2 canned green chile strips or
whole green chiles

Preheat the oven to 500 degrees. Beat the egg whites until stiff; then beat the egg yolks and fold them into the whites. Cook half the egg mixture at a time on a hot griddle for 30 to 40 seconds. Put the shredded cheese and chiles on one half and top with the other half. Transfer the stacked omelets to a baking pan and bake until the eggs are truly cooked and the cheese has melted, 10 to 15 minutes. Serve with Spanish Sauce.

This is particularly good over huevos rancheros. Also, if you prefer a hotter sauce you may substitute jalapeño peppers for the green chiles.
Makes 1 serving.

★

A stone's throw away, over in Tucson, you'll find La Fuente Restaurant, which also specializes in Mexican cuisine. They've got it all at La Fuente, from the oustanding food, to the authentic patios and other Mexican architectural touches, to a mariachi band.

☆ Tee Pee Recipe for Spanish Sauce ☆

½ cup diced white onion	¼ teaspoon ground cumin
2 tablespoons vegetable oil	⅛ teaspoon pepper
¼ teaspoon salt	1 large can diced green chiles
¼ teaspoon garlic	1 large can stewed tomatoes
¼ teaspoon paprika	1 cup chicken broth
¼ teaspoon dried oregano	1 tablespoon flour

Fry the onion in the oil over medium heat for 5 minutes. Add the spices and simmer for 3 minutes. Add green chiles, stewed tomatoes, and chicken broth. Bring to a boil. Thicken the sauce with the flour. Then simmer for 20 more minutes.
Makes 4 servings.

★

This Pastel Azteca and the La Fuente Special Tostada will give you an idea how fine Mexican food can be made rather simply if you just know how to do it.

☆ Pastel Azteca ☆

3 6-inch corn tortillas	½ avocado, sliced
3 to 4 tablespoons corn oil	3 tablespoons sour cream
1½ cups red enchilada sauce	
6 ounces breast of chicken,	
baked and shredded	

Dip the corn tortilla in the hot oil for 5 seconds. Then dip it into the enchilada sauce. Place the tortilla on a plate and layer on it the baked chicken breast, avocados, and sour cream. Repeat and top with another crisp tortilla, sour cream, and avocado.
Makes 1 serving.

☆ La Fuente Special Tostada ☆

---

1 12- to 14-inch flour tortilla
2 tablespoons shredded
  Longhorn cheese
3 tablespoons carne seca (dried
  shredded beef) or shredded
  roast beef

1 tablespoon diced onion
1 tablespoon chopped tomatoes
½ tablespoon chopped green
  chile

Place the flour tortilla on a grill and turn it frequently until crisp. Place the tortilla on a 15-inch pizza pan. Sprinkle Longhorn cheese on top, covering the entire tortilla. Spread the carne seca over the cheese. Top with the diced onion, tomatoes, and green chile. Place under the broiler until the cheese has melted. Cut into wedges and serve while hot.
Makes 1 serving.

★

Now, let's feast on a little "soul." Mrs. Frances' Kitchen (also known as Prince's Place) in Myrtle Beach, South Carolina, is the essence of soul. This small, homey roadhouse-type place has an ordinary facade that belies the savory treasures that await you within. Founded by Mrs. Frances I. Gainey Bowens, the place is packed every day for lunch, so get there early if this place is on your travel schedule.

Some of my favorites include the savory meat loaf and stewed beef dishes below. I've also included a couple of great vegetable recipes to round out either of these entrées. A lunch at Mrs. Frances' Kitchen is about three times the amount of food that any New Yorker would have for dinner.

☆ Savory Meat Loaf ☆

---

10 pounds ground beef
1 teaspoon salt
1 teaspoon pepper
1 large onion, finely chopped
1 medium-size sweet green
  pepper, finely chopped
8 medium-size eggs, beaten

1 cup instant oatmeal
½ cup all-purpose flour
2 tablespoons steak sauce
4 tablespoons prepared mustard
2 cups plus 2 tablespoons water
2 cups barbecue sauce

(Continued)

Preheat the oven to 450 degrees. Put the beef into a roasting pan; then fold and break it apart. Season with salt and pepper and fold and mix again. Add the onion and green pepper and mix again. Pour the eggs over the beef and mix until they have been absorbed into the beef. Then add the oatmeal, flour, steak sauce, and 2 tablespoons of the mustard. Mix thoroughly. After mixing for a while, push all of the beef mixture to the center of the pan, making a line of beef from one end of the pan to the other. Then roll and mold the beef into a long shape.

After log is formed, smooth out the surface by gently rolling your hand over the loaf, down the sides, and on the top, to make it as round as possible.

After you have formed the loaf as best you can, pour 2 tablespoons of water over the loaf. This will moisten the beef and allow you to shape it more easily. After shaping, pour the remaining water down each side of the loaf, spread the 2 tablespoons of the mustard over the loaf, and pour the barbecue sauce over the loaf.

Cover with aluminum foil and bake for 1 hour and 45 minutes. Cut into ½-inch-thick slices to serve. Serves 15 to 20 people depending on their appetites (closer to 15 if all are Willard-types!).
Makes 15 to 20 servings.

☆ Stewed Beef ☆

15 pounds beef chuck for stew
1 tablespoon salt
2 tablespoons pepper
½ cup all-purpose flour
4 cups cold water
2 large onions, sliced

2 large sweet green peppers, sliced
2 tablespoons A-1 Sauce
1 cup chopped mushrooms, (optional)

Preheat the oven to 500 degrees. Wash the beef, cut into 1-inch cubes, and season it with salt and pepper. Put the flour into the bottom of a large roasting pan; then add the water and mix until smooth. If the mixture is too thick, add more water.

Put half of the beef into the roaster and add half the onions and peppers. Then put in the remaining beef and onions and peppers. Pour the steak sauce over all.

Bake for 3 hours, or until the beef can be pierced with a fork. Check for dryness after 2 hours. If dry, stir in water. When just about done, you may add a cup of chopped mushrooms, if desired.
Makes 15 to 20 servings.

★

And now for some vegetable specials from Mrs. Frances' Kitchen. These are just the thing to go with the above entrées to make up the complete soul food meal.

☆ Mrs. Frances' Traditional Corn on the Cob ☆

6 to 9 ears fresh yellow corn,   Boiling water
   husked   ¼ cup (½ stick) butter

After husking, clean the corn with a fingernail brush. Put the corn into a large pot of boiling water. Add the butter and boil until corn turns golden yellow (about 30 minutes). Season to taste.
Makes 4 to 6 servings.

☆ Collards ☆

3 pounds collard greens   1 teaspoon personal seasoning
1½ cups water   (see page 164)
4 pieces ham hocks, neck bones,
   or fatback

Pick healthy small, medium, or large bunches of collard greens from your garden following the first frost. Cut off the bottom roots, wash the leaves in cold water, and cut off the thick stems. Put the meat in a skillet or pot and fry or boil with a small amount of water until done, about 30 minutes. Put the meat in a large pot and add the greens and water. Cover and boil until tender, about 1½ hours, checking to see that the water doesn't boil away.
Makes 4 to 6 servings.

☆ Okra ☆

2 pounds okra   Salt and pepper to taste
Water to cover

Wash the okra and cut off the stems. Cut the pods into ½-inch-thick slices and put in a saucepan. Add the water and salt and pepper, cover, and cook over medium heat for about 30 minutes.
Makes 6 servings.

☆ Onion Rings ☆

2 onions, peeled
Onion Batter (recipe follows)

1 cup all-purpose flour
1 cup vegetable shortening

Cut the onions into thick slices and separate them into rings. Dip the rings first into the batter and then into the flour. Dip the rings again into the batter and then into the flour two more times. Fry in the hot oil in a skillet until golden brown, about 15 minutes. Drain on paper towels.
Makes 4 to 6 servings.

Note: You can fry okra or squash the same way.

☆ Onion Batter ☆

1 large egg
½ cup all-purpose flour
¼ cup milk

1 teaspoon baking powder
Pinch each of salt and pepper

Mix all the ingredients together. The batter will be slightly lumpy.

☆ Turnips ☆

2 pounds turnips with tops

1 cup water

Wash and peel the turnips. Then cut them into cubes. Chop or shred the leaves. Put in a pot, add the water, and cover tightly. Bring to a boil; then turn the heat to medium and cook until the turnips are tender, about 30 minutes.
Serves 4.

Note: Rutabagas can be cooked this way, too.

☆ 5 ☆

King Zucchini and His Vegetable Court

Although I've liked vegetables ever since I was a kid, I've really come to *love* them in my adult years.

In part, vegetables are high on my list of table delights because I know they're good for me. Everything you read these days in health books indicates that high energy and excellent nutritional value come from "complex carbohydrates," of which vegetables are a prime example. I think they should be a key ingredient in any person's diet.

Many of the recipes in this section come from the nation's top restaurants, as do the recipes for the other types of food throughout this book. But I've also made a special effort to gather the vegetable specialties of a number of individuals who aren't necessarily connected with the food industry.

But whether they come from restaurants and professional chefs or not, these recipes will provide an excellent addition to any meal, and they can often provide you with a meal all by themselves.

I want to begin with a simple but excellent recipe for that king of all vegetables, zucchini, which pops up at many New York dinner parties. I call zucchini "the king" because it tastes so good, it's so good for you, and it has so many uses—from serving as a regular separate table vegetable, to providing the base for various breads, to being a component part of other recipes.

You'll find zucchini appearing in a number of the recipes in this book. But right now, I want to feature this royal vegetable in all its glory, with only a throne of carrots to set it off.

111

☆ New York Dinner-Party ☆
Steamed Zucchini and Carrots

---

2 carrots, julienned
2 zucchini, julienned

1 tablespoon chopped fresh
  parsley

Put the carrots, zucchini, and parsley in a vegetable steamer. Steam over simmering water in a covered pot until the vegetables are tender but *still* crunchy.
Makes 4 servings.

★

One of our research associates, Janet Ernst, was fortunate enough to find a Russian-born former chef by the name of Gary Novicky. Gary, who has also worked as a gymnastics instructor and a singer and performer at a Russian restaurant, has passed on two of his family dishes which should do wonders for any American table.

So prepare to let your taste buds transport you back to old Russia with a traditional borscht.

☆ Traditional Borscht ☆

---

2 bay leaves
1 teaspoon salt
¼ teaspoon pepper
1 celery stalk, chopped
1 16-ounce can sliced beets, or 2
  cups sliced cooked fresh beets
2 medium-size onions, chopped
3 carrots, sliced
3 potatoes, peeled and sliced
1 16-ounce can stewed tomatoes
  or sliced tomatoes, or 2 cups
  sliced fresh tomatoes
1 bunch parsley

½ bunch fresh dill
5 garlic cloves, chopped
1 14-ounce package soup greens
1 19-ounce can kidney beans
1 small head cabbage, coarsely
  chopped
¼ cup lemon juice
Sour cream to taste

Optional:
5 beef bouillon cubes
1 turnip or parsnip, peeled and
  chopped, if available

Fill a large pot one third with water. Add the bay leaves, salt, pepper, celery, beets, and onions to the pot. Bring the water to a boil, lower the heat, and simmer. Add the carrots, potatoes, tomatoes, parsley, dill, garlic, soup greens, kidney beans, cabbage, and lemon juice. Simmer for 20 minutes.

Put a dollop of sour cream on each serving. This soup tastes even better the second day.
Makes 10 servings.

★

Of course, Russians have no corner on fine vegetable cuisine. Zwan Nikolic, a former restaurant owner and New York resident whose mother taught him how to cook when he was a child in Yugoslavia, proves this point with two Yugoslavian dishes.

☆ Stuffed Peppers Yugoslavian Style ☆

2 cups *cooked* rice mixed with 8 ounces raw ground beef	Salt and pepper to taste
1 medium-size onion, diced	4 sweet green peppers, cored and seeded
2 garlic cloves	1 16-ounce can tomato purée
2 large eggs	1 tablespoon all-purpose flour

Mix the first 5 ingredients together and stuff the peppers with the mixture. Put in a pot just large enough to hold them, stuffing down. Add enough water to the pot to almost cover the peppers. Cook over medium heat until the peppers are soft.

Mix the tomato purée with 2 cups of water and add to pot. Cook for 5 to 10 minutes more. Thicken the sauce with the flour.
Makes 4 servings.

☆ Vegetables with Rice ☆

1 medium-size onion, peeled	2 celery stalks
1 medium-size carrot	1 sweet green pepper, cored
3 garlic cloves, peeled	

(Continued)

113

6 to 8 string beans with ends
trimmed
3 to 4 medium-size tomatoes
1 parsnip, peeled

¼ cup (½ stick) butter or
vegetable oil
1 cup rice
Eggplant (optional)
Cauliflower (optional)

Dice all the vegetables with a sharp knife. Melt the butter in a saucepan and add the vegetables. Stir with a wooden spoon. Then cover and cook over medium heat.

Prepare the rice (Uncle Ben's long grain preferred), following the package directions.

Add the rice to the vegetables. Cover and let stand for 5 to 10 minutes. *Makes 3 to 4 servings.*

★

To step into The Pirates' House in old Savannah, Georgia, is to step back into this country's British and American past. You get a sense of history when you visit this restaurant: Just look up onto one of the walls, where you'll see pages from a very rare edition of Robert Louis Stevenson's *Treasure Island.*

Stevenson mentioned Savannah several times in his book. In fact, by one tradition, some of the action is actually supposed to have taken place in The Pirates' House, where the buildings date back to the eighteenth century.

Herb Traub of The Pirates' House puts it this way:

" 'Tis said that old Cap'n Flint, who originally buried the fabulous treasure on Treasure Island, died here in an upstairs room. In the story, his faithful first mate, Billy Bones, was at his side when he breathed his last, muttering, 'Darby, bring aft the rum!' Even now, many swear that the ghost of Cap'n Flint still haunts The Pirates' House area on moonless nights."

Pirates, I'm sure, liked vegetables as much as the rest of us. To emphasize this point, The Pirates' House Restaurant has a tradition of serving Southern vegetable recipes that would satisfy the taste of any swashbuckler.

☆ Herbed Eggplant Casserole ☆

---

1 large or 2 small eggplant(s)
1 cup packaged onion and garlic
   croutons
1 cup grated Cheddar cheese
½ cup milk

1 tablespoon all-purpose flour
½ teaspoon salt
½ teaspoon pepper
½ teaspoon dried oregano
1 tablespoon butter

Preheat the oven to 350 degrees. Peel the eggplant and cut it into ¼-inch cubes. Cook in boiling salted water until tender; drain. Mix the eggplant, croutons, and ½ cup of the cheese in a bowl. Transfer the mixture to a lightly buttered 1-quart casserole dish. Combine the milk, flour, and seasonings in a small bowl and pour the mixture over the eggplant mixture. Top with the remaining cheese and dot with the butter. Cover and bake for 20 minutes. Uncover and continue baking for an additional 10 minutes.
Makes 4 servings.

☆ Ginger Baked Squash ☆

---

3 medium-size acorn squash,
   halved and seeded
¼ cup water
3 tablespoons butter

3 tablespoons dark brown sugar
2 tablespoons dry sherry
½ teaspoon salt
½ teaspoon ground ginger

Preheat the oven to 400 degrees. Put the squash halves, cut side down, into a baking dish. Add the water and bake for 20 minutes. Meanwhile, combine the other ingredients in a small saucepan and stir over low heat until well blended. Simmer, uncovered, for 5 minutes. Turn the squash cut side up and fill the hollows with the ginger syrup. Bake for 25 minutes longer, or until fork-tender, basting with the syrup during the last 5 minutes.
Makes 6 servings.

☆ Sweet Potato Casserole ☆

SWEET POTATOES
1 2½-pound can sweet potatoes,
   drained
1 cup sugar
¼ cup (½ stick) butter
2 large eggs
½ teaspoon salt
1 teaspoon vanilla extract
½ teaspoon ground cinnamon
½ teaspoon ground nutmeg

TOPPING
1 cup flaked coconut
1 cup firmly packed light brown
   sugar
⅓ cup self-rising flour
1 cup chopped nuts
¼ cup (½ stick) butter, melted

Preheat the oven to 350 degrees. Beat all the ingredients for the sweet potatoes together with an electric mixer or in a food processor until they are smooth. Pour into a greased 2-quart casserole.

To make the topping, mix all the topping ingredients together and spread on top of the sweet potatoes. Bake for 30 to 35 minutes.
Makes 6 to 8 servings.

☆ Fried Corn ☆

1 dozen ears corn on the cob,
   husks and silk removed
4 tablespoons bacon drippings
1 tablespoon sugar

1 teaspoon salt
Pepper to taste
Milk or cream (optional)

Slit each row of kernels down the middle lengthwise before starting to cut the corn off the cob Cut the corn from the cob with a very sharp knife into a bowl, cutting as thinly as possible and going around each ear of corn at least 2 times. Scrape the ears over the bowl with the edge of a knife after cutting off the kernels to remove all traces of milk.

Heat the bacon drippings in a heavy skillet. Add the corn. Rinse the bowl with a little water and add the water to the skillet. Add the seasonings and cook until the corn is tender, 10 to 15 minutes. Adjust the seasoning. If the corn dries out, add a little milk or cream.
Makes 10 to 12 servings.

Note: A vegetable brush removes the silks from the corn easily. Silver Queen makes the best corn for frying if you can find it, but whatever kind you use, make sure it's tender. Some people use a vegetable peeler to remove corn from cob, but it must be sharp. If you don't want to use bacon drippings, substitute ½ cup (1 stick) butter, but your corn won't have that authentic Southern taste.

☆ Succotash ☆

1 cup shelled butter beans
2 tablespoons bacon drippings
2 cups water

1 cup raw corn, cut off cob in
  large kernels
1 teaspoon salt
⅛ teaspoon pepper

Put the butter beans, bacon drippings, and water in a saucepan. Bring to a boil, lower the heat, and simmer, covered, for about 30 minutes, or until the beans are almost tender. Add the corn and cook until the beans and corn are tender, about 15 minutes. Drain and season with salt and pepper to taste and serve.
Makes 4 servings.

☆ Baked Vidalia Onions I ☆

1 Vidalia onion, or any sweet
  yellow onion, per person,
  peeled

1 tablespoon butter per onion
Salt and pepper

Preheat the oven to 350 degrees. Place each onion on a square of heavy duty aluminum foil. Add the butter and season generously; then wrap tightly. Bake for 1 hour. The onions may also be cooked, wrapped in foil, on a hot grill for 30 to 35 minutes, or until soft. Turn frequently.

☆ Baked Vidalia Onions II ☆

Vidalia onions, peeled
Instant beef granules

Seasoned salt and pepper
1 teaspoon butter per onion

(*Continued*)

117

Preheat the oven to 350 degrees. Place 1 to 2 onions per person in a baking dish. Sprinkle with the beef granules, seasoned salt, and pepper. Top with the butter. Cover tightly with aluminum foil and bake for 1 hour.

☆ Savannah Hoppin' John ☆

2 cups dried red peas or cow peas	Ham hocks or neck bone
5 cups cold water	Pepper and Tabasco sauce to taste
1 medium-size onion, chopped	1 cup rice
2 tablespoons bacon drippings	1 teaspoon salt

Sort and wash the beans and soak in the cold water to cover for 8 hours or overnight. In a heavy pot, sauté the onion in the bacon drippings until soft. Add beans and water, meat, pepper, and Tabasco to taste.

Bring to a boil, lower the heat, cover, and simmer until the beans are soft, 1 to 1½ hours. Stir in the rice and 1 teaspoon salt. Cover and simmer for 20 minutes, or until the rice is tender. If the mixture is too wet, remove the lid and simmer until the desired consistency is reached. Taste and adjust the seasonings.
Makes about 6 servings.

☆ Hoppin' John ☆

1 pound dried black-eyed peas	1 teaspoon salt
6 cups cold water	2 medium-size onions, chopped
8 ounces slab bacon, cut into 1-inch cubes	1 cup rice
1 teaspoon Tabasco sauce	1½ cups boiling water

Sort and wash the peas. Put the peas in a large pot with the cold water. Bring to a boil and boil for 2 minutes. Cover, remove from the heat, and let sit for 1 hour.

In a frying pan, cook the bacon slowly until it is brown on all sides; use tongs to turn the bacon. Reserve the bacon drippings and add the bacon, Tabasco sauce, and salt to the peas. Bring to a boil, lower the heat, and simmer, covered, for 30 minutes.

Sauté the onions in the reserved bacon drippings until they are translucent. Add the onions to the peas. Stir in the rice and boiling water. Cover and simmer, stirring occasionally, for 30 minutes, or until the rice is tender. It should be moist, but not wet, and most certainly not dry. Taste for seasoning; you will probably need more salt.
Makes about 6 servings.

Note: Hoppin' John is traditionally eaten in the South on New Year's Day to bring luck in the coming year. You may substitute fatback for the bacon, but the flavor will not be as good.

☆ Okra, Corn, and Tomatoes ☆

1 pound fresh okra, or 1 1-lb bag
   frozen okra
4 to 6 ears fresh corn, or 1
   10-ounce box frozen corn
4 slices bacon
1 medium-size onion, sliced
2 tablespoons bacon drippings
   (optional)

1 1-pound can tomatoes
Half of a 6-ounce can tomato
   paste
1 teaspoon sugar
Salt and pepper to taste

Wash the okra and cut off the stem ends; then cut the pods into ½-inch-thick slices. Cut the corn kernels off the cobs. Fry the bacon in a heavy skillet until crisp; remove the bacon and drain on paper towels. Crumble when cool.

Fry the onion in the bacon drippings until it is soft. Add the okra and cook for 2 to 3 minutes, stirring occasionally. (You may want to add more bacon drippings.)

Drain the tomato liquid into the pan with the okra and squeeze the tomatoes through your fingers into the pan. Add the tomato paste, corn, crumbled bacon, and sugar. Lower the heat, cover, and cook until done, 15 to 20 minutes. Season with salt and pepper and serve.
Makes 3 to 4 servings.

Note: The okra mixture, without the corn, is good served over rice. If you don't want to fry bacon, just use bacon drippings you have on hand.

★

It's been said that potatoes are the perfect food. I find myself ready and willing to believe this statement after salivating over this London Chop House recipe for Potato Pancakes.

☆ Potato Pancakes ☆

1 large Idaho potato	2 tablespoons chopped onion
2 tablespoons all-purpose flour	Salt and pepper to taste
1 teaspoon baking powder	Clarified butter
1 large egg	

Grate the potato using a medium grater; then wash three times in running cold water, pressing the excess out each time. Dry completely with paper towels. Mix the potato with the flour, baking powder, egg, and onion. Season with salt and pepper. Shape into 3-inch *very thin* pancakes. Sauté over high heat in the butter until golden brown and crisp on both sides. Drain on paper towels.
Makes 24 3-inch pancakes.

★

For the ultimate German version of potato pancakes, you should try these from Mader's Restaurant in Milwaukee. Then, if you really want to make a German veggie meal out of it, include Mader's Red Cabbage, Carrots, and Cucumber Salad.

☆ Kartoffelpfannkuchen (Potato Pancakes) ☆

2 large Idaho potatoes	About 3 tablespoons cracker
Milk	meal
1 teaspoon grated onion	Vegetable oil for frying
1 large egg	Apple sauce

Peel the potatoes and grate, using a fine grater. Drain thoroughly through several thicknesses of cheesecloth and measure the water. Replace with milk. Add the onion and egg mixed with about 3 tablespoons of cracker meal. Shape it into pancakes and cook in ¼ inch of hot

vegetable oil until nicely browned on both sides. Serve immediately with hot apple sauce.
Makes 4 to 5 servings.

☆ German Braised Red Cabbage ☆

This dish, based on a Swiss recipe, can be reheated very easily if desired. It is also excellent with pork.

1 1½-pound red cabbage
1 tablespoon butter or lard
1 onion, finely chopped
2 tablespoons dry red wine or
   water

1 cooking apple, peeled, cored,
   and chopped
1 teaspoon sugar
1 teaspoon red wine vinegar
Salt and pepper to taste

Wash and drain cabbage and cut it into shreds, removing the coarse outer leaves and core. Melt the butter and brown the onion lightly. Add the cabbage and cook for a few minutes, turning frequently.

Add the remaining ingredients, bring to a boil, and simmer, covered, until the cabbage is tender and almost all the liquid has cooked away. The cabbage should still be a little crisp. This will take about 45 minutes.
Makes 5 to 6 servings.

☆ Rheinlaendische (Rhineland Style Carrots) ☆

1 pound carrots, peeled and
   diced (about 2¼ cups)
1 teaspoon sugar
½ teaspoon salt
2 tablespoons butter
3 medium-size onions, thinly
   sliced

½ cup carrot cooking liquid
3 tart apples, peeled, cored, and
   cut into eighths
Pepper to taste

Cook the carrots in boiling water to just cover, adding the sugar and salt. When the carrots are almost tender, remove them from the heat, drain, and reserve ½ cup of the liquid.

(Continued)

Melt the butter, add the onions, and cook, stirring, until transparent but not brown. Add the carrots, cooking liquid, and apple. Cover and cook gently until the carrots and apples are tender.
Makes 5 to 6 servings.

☆ Gurkensalat (Cucumber Salad) ☆

1 long slender cucumber
1 teaspoon salt
3 tablespoons white vinegar
3 teaspoons sugar
Freshly ground pepper to taste

1 scallion, finely sliced
½ cup sour cream
2 tablespoons finely minced
   parsley

If the cucumber skin isn't tender, peel and score it lengthwise with the tines of a fork. Slice the cucumber very thin. Sprinkle with the salt, cover, and refrigerate for several minutes.

Meanwhile, mix the vinegar, sugar, pepper, and scallion in a bowl. Stir in the sour cream.

Press the moisture from the cucumbers, draining thoroughly. Add the dressing, mix well, and transfer to a small bowl. Garnish with the minced parsley
Makes 5 to 6 servings.

★

Are you a person who prefers a steak sandwich or a big slab of roast beef three times a day, seven days a week? Even if you are, you'll be enthralled by the vegetable platter at Woods Restaurant and Bar in Manhattan. This is probably the best, most complete vegetarian platter that you can find anywhere in the world. It's a real gourmet's delight.

When I've eaten at Woods, I've seen all sorts of well-known people there—celebrities like Hume Cronyn, Jessica Tandy, and Bill Murray—partaking of lunch or dinner. The folks at Woods passed on one story to me about an incident involving a well-known female singer and her fiancé who had come into Woods for lunch.

"They spotted the press outside our front window and begged for a way out," a member of the Woods staff told me. "But there really is no other way out to the street. So I finally arranged with M. J. Knouds, the riding and saddlery shop next door, for a way out."

So the singer and her fiancé, accompanied by a guide from Woods, went back through the kitchen, out into the backyard, over some boxes, and into the Knouds' backyard. Then they proceeded over some more boxes and into the Knouds' stockroom. Finally, the couple moved to the front of the store and waited there for an opportune time to make their escape.

Such is life when you're living in the fast lane and eating in the fine restaurants of Manhattan! You can get your own personal taste of the excitement with this vegetable platter.

☆ Woods Steamed Vegetable Platter ☆

1 yam
2 carrots, julienned
2 zucchini, sliced thin on the diagonal
1 yellow squash, sliced thin on the diagonal
1 sweet yellow pepper
1 beet
1 acorn squash
Ground cinnamon to taste
Dark brown sugar to taste
1 artichoke
8 brussels sprouts (2 per plate)
20 string beans (5 per plate)
½ head cauliflower

4 to 8 cherry tomatoes (1 or 2 per plate)
Purée: kohlrabi, white turnip, potatoes, corn, 1 cup (2 sticks) butter, 1 cup heavy cream, salt, pepper, minced red pepper
1 head broccoli
2 leeks (½ a leek per plate)
½ red cabbage
½ white cabbage
1 head kale (1 large leaf per plate)

First, bake the yam at 350 to 400 degrees until it is soft, at least 1 hour. While the yam is baking, prepare the other vegetables as appropriate: Wash everything and trim if necessary. Cut the carrots into sticks. Slice both zucchini and yellow squash thin on the diagonal. Cut the yellow pepper into 4 rings. Put the beet on to boil for 30 minutes. Bake the acorn squash for 25 to 35 minutes, with cinnamon and brown sugar to taste. Also starting about this time cook the artichoke for 20 minutes.

While the yam, beet, acorn squash, and artichoke are cooking, lightly poach the brussels sprouts, string beans, cauliflower, cherry tomatoes, and yellow pepper. To do this, bring a pot of water to a low boil, with a bit of butter and salt. Put each vegetable in the boiling water very briefly —about half a minute for most, up to maybe 1½ minutes for the yellow pepper. *(Continued)*

123

When the yam, beet, acorn squash, and artichoke are done, allow each to cool and then slice, cube, or quarter as you prefer.

Prepare the purée, which consists of kohlrabi, white turnip, potatoes, corn, 1 cup (2 sticks) of butter, 1 cup of heavy cream, salt, pepper, and red pepper. Boil the first 3 ingredients together until they're soft. Add the corn and cook until it's soft. Drain off all water. Blend with a bit of butter, cream, salt, and pepper. Repeat, stir, and add the minced red pepper.

Briefly steam the carrots and broccoli over orange- and celery-flavored water. Then add all vegetables to the steamer, starting with those that take longer to steam, and ending up with the quick things like the kale leaves on top. Steam for 2 minutes. Then arrange the vegetables neatly on each plate, putting the cabbage into the center, topping it with the yellow pepper and cherry tomatoes. The purée is served on top of each steamed kale leaf.
Makes 4 servings.

Junior League Vegetables

One of the most important ingredients in my travels to the many towns and cities in this country is the relationship I've developed with the Junior League.

Members of the Junior League often have their roots in old, established American families. So when you enjoy a Junior League recipe, you're really participating firsthand in some of the best, most historic gourmet cooking that America has to offer.

As a whole, I've found the various Junior League local cookbooks to be the best in the country. Sometimes, you'll even be lucky enough to find one of their secret recipes which hasn't yet been published. To show you what I mean, try these previously unpublished vegetable specialties from the Junior League of the City of New York.

☆ Stuffed Tomatoes ☆

1½ pounds mushrooms, cleaned and finely chopped	1 tablespoon diced truffles
1 shallot, chopped	1 teaspoon chopped parsley
2 tablespoons butter	½ teaspoon salt
2 tablespoons tomato purée or gravy	6 tomatoes with cores and seeds removed, drained
	½ cup bread crumbs, buttered

Preheat the oven to 350 degrees. In a skillet, sauté the mushrooms and shallot in the butter until all the moisture has evaporated.

Add the tomato purée, truffles, parsley, and salt. Fill the tomato shells with the stuffing, top them with buttered bread crumbs, and arrange them in a well-buttered shallow casserole. Bake for 20 minutes. *Makes 6 servings.*

☆ Black-Eyed Bean (Pea) Salad ☆

4 cups diced black-eyed beans, sorted and washed
1 medium-size onion

¼ cup chopped coriander
1 garlic clove, minced
Salt and pepper to taste

Cover the beans with water and bring to a boil; boil for 2 minutes. Remove from the heat and let soak for 1 hour. Bring the beans to a boil and cook for about 45 minutes, or until they are tender but firm. Let them cool completely. Chop the onion and add it to the drained beans with the coriander and garlic. Season with salt and pepper. Serve on a bed of lettuce or Boston lettuce with oil and vinegar to taste or vinaigrette dressing.
Makes 8 servings.

☆ Cauliflower in Hot Vinegar ☆

1 small cauliflower
2 tablespoons olive oil
2 garlic cloves
1 teaspoon paprika

2 tablespoons white wine vinegar
2 tablespoons cauliflower cooking liquid

Wash the cauliflower and cut it into flowerets. Simmer the cauliflower in plenty of boiling salted water for 10 minutes, or until it is nearly tender. Reserve 2 tablespoons of the cooking liquid; then drain the cauliflower.

Meanwhile, heat the oil in a small saucepan. Fry the garlic cloves until they are lightly browned. Discard the garlic. Remove the saucepan from the heat and stir in the paprika, vinegar, and cooking liquid. Put the cauliflower in a saucepan and pour the vinegar sauce over the cauliflower. Cover and simmer over very low heat for 5 to 10 minutes.
Makes 4 servings.

☆ Sweet Beets ☆

---

1 tablespoon cornstarch	¼ cup honey
½ teaspoon salt	2 tablespoons butter
1 tablespoon beet cooking liquid	2 cups cooked, peeled, and diced
2 tablespoons red wine vinegar	beets

Mix the cornstarch and salt together in a saucepan; then blend in the beet juice. Add the vinegar, honey, and butter. Cook slowly over medium heat, stirring constantly, until thick. Pour over the drained beets and allow to stand for at least 10 minutes to absorb the flavor. Reheat and serve.
Makes 4 servings.

★

Now, let's try a simple but quite elegant preparation of one of the healthiest *and* tastiest vegetables of all—broccoli. If zucchini is the king, then broccoli must be the crown prince of vegetables. But it's only tasty when it's cooked lightly. There's nothing worse than overcooked, soggy broccoli.

With this recipe, which is used by a number of gourmet cooks I know, you'll always come up a crunchy winner with your broccoli servings.

☆ Stir-Fried Broccoli ☆

---

1 bunch broccoli	½ cup water
2 to 3 tablespoons corn oil	½ cup soy sauce

Slice the broccoli across the flowerets and stems to make bite-size pieces. In a wok or frying pan, heat the oil and add broccoli, stirring quickly. After a minute or so, add the water and soy sauce. Cover and cook over high heat for a couple of minutes, or until the broccoli is slightly cooked, but still crunchy; do not let it overcook. Remove from the heat and transfer to a serving dish.
Makes 4 to 6 servings.

★

Le Pèrigord Park Restaurant has a very sophisticated New York dining room, yet unlike many other high-class Manhattan eating places, there's a family atmosphere. Although there are touches of formality here and there, such as the way the waiters wait on you hand and foot, the place projects an atmosphere of warmth that many other gourmet restaurants lack. That's a major reason I like Le Pèrigord Park. Their Sauce Vinaigrette is a great addition to any vegetable dish.

☆ Sauce Vinaigrette ☆

1 tablespoon red wine vinegar
1 tablespoon Dijon mustard
½ teaspoon salt

½ teaspoon white pepper
4 tablespoons olive oil

Mix together the vinegar, mustard, salt, and pepper. Then slowly add the olive oil. If the sauce is too thick, add some water. Serve with asparagus, artichokes, salad, or your favorite vegetable.
Makes 4 to 5 servings.

★

As I mentioned earlier, the Gourmet House in Bismarck, North Dakota, has many specialties to commend, not the least of which was that pecan pie that I carried on an airplane down to the *Phil Donahue Show*. But there are a lot of things that lead up to the Gourmet House's dessert menu. One favorite, the just-right thing for salad buffs, is their Blue Cheese Dressing.

☆ Blue Cheese Dressing ☆

1 pint (2 cups) heavy cream
10 ounces blue cheese,
   crumbled
¼ cup chopped chives

1 teaspoon Worcestershire sauce
Dash of Tabasco sauce
¼ teaspoon garlic salt
Freshly ground pepper to taste

Whip the cream and then fold in the blue cheese, chives, Worcestershire sauce, Tabasco sauce, garlic salt, and pepper. Cover and chill well.
Makes 2 pints.

★

The Mad Hatter, a little jewel of a restaurant which faces the Gulf on Sanibel Island, Florida, offers a variety of great fish dishes and other tantalizing entrées. But one of the key ingredients which distinguishes any meal at the Hatter is their fabulous house dressing.

☆ The Mad Hatter's House Dressing ☆

1 gallon mayonnaise
⅕ jar honey (4-pound jar)
8 medium-to-large shallots, minced

⅕ cup chopped parsley
4 ounces Dijon mustard
1 quart milk

Mix all the ingredients together and let sit for 24 hours. *Makes 80 servings.*

☆ 6 ☆

Soup's On!

In my little world of fantasy, as I sit and stare off into space, I frequently have this image of the New England coast, with a dramatic, craggy, rocky shore and a lighthouse in the distance. The waves are lashing about, the wind is blowing at a good clip, and the temperature registers about 35 degrees.

Then somehow, I end up inside the lighthouse, where a big kettle of clam chowder or some other aromatic seafood concoction is bubbling away on the hearth. Whatever problems I may have begin to melt away as this daydream intensifies. And I know that the key to my growing sense of well-being is that tantalizing soup.

I'm sure that a psychiatrist could make a great deal of such a flight of the imagination. This mental "movie" usually begins to run in times when I'm particularly reflective, say, in a state of depression, fatigue, or just a philosophical reverie.

I even *dream* about soup sometimes. My mother used to make cream of potato soup when I was a kid, especially when I was sick. I think some of those eating experiences must have become embedded in my mind in a way that gives me special feelings of comfort and security when I'm thinking seriously about my life. I can actually remember the aromas and tastes of the little pieces of onion and celery that would go into her recipes.

Soups were always an important part of our home life. We might have a piece of roast beef or a ham, but we'd never waste anything, especially not when there was a possibility of turning some of the leftovers into a tasty broth. We'd take the bone that was left over and make a nice beef or ham stock. Then, we'd combine it with some fresh vegetables for a special Scott vegetable soup. Or we might use black beans or split peas for the main ingredient.

I don't think there's anything as filling or as comforting as a good bowl of soup. It's truly the all-purpose food, both physically and emotionally. Soup and a salad, soup and a sandwich, soup by itself—whatever the combination, I love it. So in the next few pages, join with me in my special hot, liquid love affair with this appetizer.

★

There's a romantic old story at The Cloister on Sea Island, Georgia, which just happens to be true—though now it's approaching the annals of offshore legend.

The Cloister, among other things, is famous for many of its fine liquid-type dishes, such as soups and sauces. It seems that in days gone by there were "sauce passers" who moved around serving sauces to the different guests.

On one occasion, a pretty young sauce passer found herself serving a handsome army officer. But all did not go well at first. As the man sat there in his uniformed finery, she somehow managed to drop a large blob of sauce smack dab on his tie. It was shocking at first, to say the least. But then the shock turned to love at first sight as their eyes met.

The officer and the sauce passer eventually married, and their daughter currently works on The Cloister chamber staff!

It would be easy to imagine something equally romantic and memorable happening with some of The Cloister's fine soup dishes, a number of which are described in detail below.

☆ Crab Bisque ☆

¾ cup (1½ sticks) butter
1 cup diced celery
1 cup diced onion
2 garlic cloves, chopped
2 bay leaves
1 tablespoon dried thyme
1 heaping tablespoon fresh
  rosemary leaves, or 1
  teaspoon dried rosemary
  leaves

1 cup all-purpose flour
4 cups strong chicken stock
4 cups fish stock
½ cup tomato paste
½ cup dry white wine
Dash of Tabasco sauce
1 tablespoon lemon juice
1 tablespoon sugar
1 pint half-and-half
1 cup heavy cream

8 ounces lump crab meat
3 tablespoons monosodium
glutamate (optional)

½ cup dry sherry
Brandy to taste
Salt and pepper to taste

Melt the butter in a soup pot; add the celery, onion, garlic, bay leaves, thyme, and rosemary. Cook the vegetables until light brown. Then add the flour, stir, and cook a little longer. Add the stocks, tomato paste, white wine, Tabasco sauce, lemon juice, and sugar and bring to a boil. Stir and simmer for about 1 hour. Remove from the heat and strain through a fine sieve into a clean pot. Add the half-and-half, heavy cream, crab meat, monosodium glutamate, sherry, and brandy and stir well. Heat briefly, but do not boil. Season with salt and pepper.
Makes 20 servings.

☆ The Cloister's Melon Soup ☆

1 quart sour cream
3 large *ripe* melons (overripe is
best), peeled, seeded, and
cubed

1 quart half-and-half
1 cup sugar
1 cup fresh lemon juice

Purée all the ingredients in a blender, in batches, if necessary. Transfer to a bowl, cover, and chill.
Makes 16 to 18 servings.

Note: If honeydew is used, add 12 to 15 fresh mint leaves.

☆ The Cloister's Cucumber Soup ☆

2½ cups water
3 cucumbers, peeled (reserve
skins)
1 small onion, chopped
¾ cup butter
1 tablespoon salt
1 teaspoon pepper
1 teaspoon fresh dillweed
1 chicken bouillon cube
½ cup flour
White pepper to taste

Monosodium glutamate to taste
1 tablespoon lemon juice
5 to 6 drops Worcestershire
sauce
Approximately 1 cup milk, half-
and-half, or sour cream
1 cucumber, peeled, seeded, and
puréed (optional)
Sprinkle of chopped parsley
Sprinkle of fresh dillweed

Bring the cucumber skins to a boil in 2½ cups of water. Simmer for 10 minutes; then strain and discard the skins. Set the stock aside.

Cut fleshy part of the cucumbers into julienne strips and set aside.

Use the center part of the cucumber (with seeds). Cut into ½-inch cubes. Sauté cucumber and onion in ¼ cup butter. When half-cooked, add the salt, pepper, dillweed (*not seed*), and chicken bouillon cubes. Sauté for 10 more seconds.

Add the reserved cucumber stock and simmer for 5 minutes. Prepare a roux by combining remaining butter and flour. Strain the stock and rub some of the remaining cucumber and onion through the sieve. Thicken with the roux blanc and bring to a boil. Season with salt, white pepper, monosodium glutamate, lemon juice, and Worcestershire Sauce to taste. Add cucumber julienne and chill thoroughly.

Then adjust thickness by adding milk, half-and-half, or sour cream. (Because flavor changes between hot and cold soup, be sure to taste and season again, after chilling.) You may also improve the soup by adding the pulp of an uncooked, peeled, and deseeded cucumber (puréed in a blender!) for freshness. Serve well chilled; sprinkle some chopped parsley and/or fresh dillweed over the soup.
Makes 8 servings.

★

This gumbo, which is one of the things which has made Wintzell's Oyster House in Mobile, Alabama, famous, can rival similar dishes in Louisiana or any other part of the country. This particular recipe, by the way, is relatively simple. It has fewer ingredients than you'll find in "heavier" gumbos, such as the one that we'll consider a few pages later from Colonial Williamsburg.

☆ "Gumbo" ☆

4 tablespoons all-purpose flour
4 tablespoons lard
1 large onion, chopped
1 large sweet green pepper, chopped
1 cup diced celery
2 garlic cloves, minced

3 quarts boiling water
4 beef or chicken bouillon cubes
Salt and pepper and cayenne pepper, if desired, to taste
1 quart oysters
1 tablespoon *filé* powder

Cook the flour in the lard until it is golden brown, stirring constantly to prevent burning or lumping. Add half of the onion, green pepper, celery, and garlic and sauté for about 1 minute. Add this mixture to the 3 quarts of boiling water and mix thoroughly.

Then add the bouillon cubes and the remaining onion, green pepper, celery, and garlic and simmer for at least 30 minutes. Season with salt and pepper. Add the oysters and cook for 3 to 5 minutes. Remove from the heat, add *filé* powder, and mix well.

Let the soup sit, covered, for at least 15 minutes. Serve over boiled rice. This can be used as the base for any seafood gumbo.
Makes 4 to 6 servings.

★

America's finest restaurants offer a lot of surprises such as serving superior dishes which are really supposed to be the specialties of another part of the country. As a case in point, take New England clam chowder. You'd think that the best recipes could only come from New England, right? Wrong! To prove it, I want you to try this New England Clam Chowder from The Mucky Duck restaurant on Captiva Island, Florida.

☆ Homemade Mucky Duck ☆ New England Clam Chowder

1 medium-size onion, chopped	1 8-ounce bottle clam juice
¾ cup chopped celery	1 gallon milk
3 large potatoes, washed and cut into ½-inch cubes	1½ cups (3 sticks) butter
	½ cup all-purpose flour
2 to 3 clams or 1 8-ounce can chopped clams in juice (depending how clam-y you like it)	White pepper, salt, dried thyme, and seafood seasoning to taste

Put the onion, celery, potatoes, and all the clam juice, including the juice from the chopped clams, in a large pot. Simmer together until the potatoes are soft. Add the clams and the milk and simmer while you prepare a roux.

(Continued)

To make the roux, melt the butter in a saucepan and stir in the flour, stirring until the roux is thick, like a milk shake, and smooth. Leave on the stove over *very* low heat for a short while.

Now it's time to season the chowder. Add a good shot of white pepper, some salt, dried thyme shaken over the chowder pot covering at least half of the top, and a little less seafood seasoning. Now add your roux slowly as you stir constantly until the chowder is thick. Remove from the heat. If the chowder gets too thick when you serve, add milk before you heat it again.
Makes 8 servings.

★

The thing I remember most about the Wayside Inn in Middletown, Virginia, is their Peanut Soup. Most people I run into who are unfamiliar with peanut country aren't even aware that peanuts can be made into soup! But I assure you, this is a dish you won't forget. I've also thrown in a couple of their other soup specialties for good measure.

☆ Peanut Soup ☆

3½ cups chicken broth or stock
1 celery stalk, chopped
1 medium-size carrot, chopped
1 small onion, chopped

1 cup creamy peanut butter
1 13-ounce can evaporated milk
  or light cream
Pinch of sugar

In a large saucepan, combine the broth, celery, carrot, and onion. Bring to a boil and lower the heat. Cover and simmer for 15 minutes, or until the vegetables are tender. Strain into a bowl, discarding the vegetables.

In the same saucepan, gradually stir the hot broth into the peanut butter. (The mixture may be stiff at first, but it will become smooth.) Add the evaporated milk and sugar. Heat through, but do not boil.
Makes 6 servings.

☆ Wine and Cheese Soup ☆

5½ cups trimmed, rinsed, and
thinly sliced leeks
¼ cup (½ stick) butter
3 cups chicken broth
3 cups water
½ cup elbow macaroni, coarsely
crushed and cooked until
tender

1 cup shredded Jarlsberg or
Swiss cheese
1 cup Chablis or dry white wine

In a 4-quart saucepan over medium heat, cook the leeks in the hot butter until tender, about 20 minutes. Add the broth and water and bring to a boil. Turn the heat to low and add the macaroni, cheese, and wine. Heat, stirring, until the cheese melts. Garnish with additional cheese, if desired.
Makes 9 servings.

☆ Potato-Leek Soup ☆

2½ pounds potatoes, peeled and
thinly sliced
1 pound onions, thinly sliced
1½ pounds white part of leeks,
washed well and thinly sliced

16 cups chicken stock
Salt and pepper to taste
2 tablespoons chopped parsley

Combine all ingredients *except* the parsley and bring to a boil. Lower the heat and simmer for about 1 hour, or until all the ingredients are soft. Purée in batches in a food processor and adjust the seasonings.
Pour into soup bowls and sprinkle each portion with chopped parsley.
Makes 10 to 12 servings.

★

There are many different ways to make Gumbo. But if I've got some time and I'm pretty hungry—and I've also got a number of other people that I'd like to serve—I think it's hard to beat this chilled crab gumbo from the Colonial Williamsburg Inn.

135

☆ Williamsburg Inn Chilled Crab Gumbo ☆

Bouquet garni of 6 parsley
stems, chopped; 1 garlic
clove, minced; ½ teaspoon
dried thyme; ½ teaspoon
dried marjoram; and 2 bay
leaves
½ cup finely chopped celery
½ cup finely chopped onion
½ cup finely chopped sweet
green pepper
½ cup finely chopped well-
washed leeks

1 pound crab meat, cooked
Pinch of saffron threads
1 cup chopped okra (see Note)
1 cup chopped tomatoes
1 teaspoon salt, or to taste
½ teaspoon white pepper
½ teaspoon *filé* powder (see
Note)
1 packet unflavored gelatin
softened in ½ cup warm water
1 cup rice, cooked

Prepare a bouquet garni by tying the herbs in a cheesecloth bag. Bring 2 quarts of water to a boil and add the bouquet garni, celery, onion, green pepper, and leeks. Cover and simmer for 20 minutes.

Pick over the crab meat and remove any bits of shell or cartilage.

Add the crab meat and saffron to the simmering vegetables and continue to simmer for 15 minutes.

Add the okra, tomatoes, salt, and pepper.

Remove ½ cup of the liquid from the soup pot, sprinkle in the *filé* powder, and beat thoroughly.

Then stir this mixture back into the soup. *Be careful not to let the soup boil after the* filé *powder has been added or it will become stringy and unfit to serve.*

Remove from the heat and stir in the softened gelatin.

Add the cooked rice and adjust the seasonings.

Refrigerate overnight, if possible, to bring out the flavor. Serve in cold cups.

Makes 12 servings.

Note: If canned okra is used, the liquid should be added to the gumbo after the cooking process because it will enhance the flavor of the soup. If raw okra is used, blanch it in 2 cups of the stock before adding it to the gumbo.

Okra will take the place of *filé* powder if the latter is not available; however, gumbo tastes better when both okra and *filé* powder are used.

Soup's On!

★

One of the unsung, hidden little gems in Manhattan is Bis! Restaurant —and perhaps the most memorable part of its menu is its soups.

The warmth of the place is probably best illustrated in this story that Narcisse S. Cadgene, the owner, tells about an evening that my wife Mary and I spent there:

"The average New Yorker probably doesn't know any more people than the average person in any other town in the United States. But the big difference lies in just how many of those little circles of friends come to exist, and how often they may overlap.

"Nothing illustrates this theory at Bis! better than an encounter we had with Willard Scott. Willard and Mary were on their dessert course at one table. Three of my friends were at another table, and, nearby, two other people were ordering entrées.

"I was supposed to be working, but it was late, so I took the opportunity to sit down to chat. Somebody made a friendly crack about my quitting early, and Willard chimed in with something that set everyone, staff included, laughing.

"At that moment the door opened and two more friends of the restaurant breezed in for dessert. One of them peered at the Scott table for a second and said, 'Aren't you Willard Scott? We met at the Coliseum two months ago when you helped us on a Junior League tennis benefit.'

"Suddenly, the mood of the restaurant changed; instead of four separate tables, we had a dinner party for ten on our hands."

I think this story says as much about the warmth of Bis! as anything, except perhaps for the "housewife's" soup and some of the other recipes which follow.

☆ Potage Ménagère (Housewife's Soup) ☆

3 large or 5 small leeks
1 bunch celery, leaves only
1 cup shredded cabbage
2 to 3 tablespoons butter
1 garlic clove, crushed
3 cups chicken stock
2 to 3 tomatoes, peeled and chopped, or 1 12-ounce can of tomatoes with juice, chopped

1 bay leaf
2 pinches of dried thyme
Pinch of dried tarragon
Salt and pepper to taste
1 cup grated Swiss, Muenster, mozzarella, or Monterey Jack cheese

(Continued)

137

Cut leeks in half lengthwise, wash well, and thinly julienne the bottom white parts. (Save the green tops for your next stock.) Chop equally finely the celery leaves. Cut the cabbage shreds into 1-inch lengths.

In a good-size saucepan, melt the butter. Add the leeks, celery leaves, and cabbage to the pan. Sauté the vegetables over low to medium heat, stirring often. When done, they should be very limp but not brown. Just before the vegetables are done, add the garlic. Cook for another 2 to 3 minutes over low heat; then remove the garlic.

Add to the pot the chicken stock, tomatoes, bay leaf, thyme, tarragon, salt, and pepper.

Cover and simmer for about 30 minutes. Adjust the seasonings. Serve hot and pass the grated cheese at the table for those who want to sprinkle it on top.

Makes 4 servings.

☆ Walnut Soup ☆

Though the walnut flavor comes through, the seasonings in this soup "marry" so subtly that it will keep everyone guessing as to what's in it.

1½ cups coarsely chopped
 walnuts
4 cups chicken stock
1 garlic clove, chopped
1 to 2 teaspoons curry power

1 bay leaf
1 teaspoon salt
¼ teaspoon pepper
½ to 1 cup heavy cream

Put the walnuts, 1 cup of the chicken stock, and the garlic in a blender. Blend until the walnuts are very fine but not puréed.

Pour the nut mixture into a saucepan and add the remaining chicken stock, curry powder, bay leaf, salt, and pepper. Simmer for 30 minutes, or until the walnut bits are very tender. Just before serving, add the heavy cream. Then return to the heat briefly, but do not boil. Adjust the seasonings. Thin the soup with a little more chicken stock, if necessary.

Makes 4 servings.

★

To my mind, the thing that really makes a good chicken soup is clarity of the broth and just enough but not too much salt. Also, it can't be too greasy.

Some people think of chicken soup as being mainly a Jewish dish. But of course, that's not true. Go to a Chinese restaurant, and what's the first thing that they put in front of you? Often, it's some sort of chicken soup, maybe chicken broth and rice.

There's also a growing recognition in scientific circles that chicken soup has medicinal value. In fact, some hospitals are even canning their own chicken soup! There's strength in the broth, it's easy to digest, it's nourishing, and it's warm and comforting. Not only that, there seems to be some sort of "X" factor in chicken soup that sets it apart from all others.

Perhaps my most significant encounter with chicken soup was while I was doing a television pilot called *Willard's World,* which we were hoping would become a regular, syndicated TV program. It was supposed to be like another *Arthur Godfrey Show,* but unfortunately, it just didn't work. Our effort became one of those "fallen soufflés" of the American entertainment world.

But there was one major bright spot. One of the things we wanted to do on the program was to find the ultimate chicken soup recipe. A number of people submitted candidates, but the cook who finally came out on top was a woman by the name of Esther Brandice of New York City.

We put a big pot of her soup out for the TV crew, and, before I knew it, there was only half a cup left for me!

But I was eternally grateful that I got that half cup. It was the greatest chicken soup I'd ever tasted. It almost didn't matter that as that wonderful soup slipped down my throat, the television show simultaneously slipped out of my hands. In any case, here's Esther's great recipe.

☆ Esther's Famous Chicken Soup ☆

1 4½- to 5-pound soup chicken, quartered
2 garlic cloves
3 medium-size onions, diced
Fresh dill and parsley leaves to taste
2 parsnips, peeled and diced
4 celery stalks, diced
4 large carrots, diced

Soup greens (but no turnip), cut up
1 tablespoon kosher salt
¼ teaspoon pepper
1 tablespoon dried dill
Pinch of garlic powder
1 pound fine egg noodles (Goodman's is best), cooked

(Continued)

139

Wash the chicken in cold water. Get rid of the fine membranes from under the skin and cut away the excess fat from around and under the skin. Rub the garlic cloves on the bottom and sides of a 10-quart aluminum pot.

Then fill the pot three quarters of the way with cold water. Add the chicken quarters and all the cut-up vegetables to the water.

Tie the loose greens with white thread and place on top of all other vegetables. Bring to a boil and add all the remaining ingredients (except for egg noodles). Lower the heat so that the water is just simmering and cover the pot.

Cook the soup for 1 hour, or until the carrots and chicken drumstick are tender. (A little tasting of the soup can't hurt.) Remove the soup greens, vegetables, and chicken (see Note), and strain the soup through a fine strainer into a clean pot. Serve with egg noodles. The mashed or sliced cooked carrots and parsnips in the soup add an extra nourishing and delicious touch. Finally, enjoy in good health!
Makes 10 to 12 servings.

Note: The chicken can be served separately, or used in another dish.

☆ 7 ☆

Willard's Best Breads
and Breakfasts

Some people think it's best to eat a meal without any bread, but I definitely don't belong to that school!

As far as I'm concerned, there's something about a piece of bread, a muffin, or some other bakery product that adds a special touch to any meal—and that's especially true of breakfast. Whoever heard of a decent breakfast without a piece of toast, a roll, or a muffin?

So we'll start out here with some of my all-time favorite bread and bakery dishes, foods that will absolutely crumble in your hand and melt in your mouth. Then, here and there, I'll slip in some breakfast highlights that I've been fortunate enough to savor in different parts of the country.

☆ Nancy Reagan's Monkey Bread ☆

During the 1981 Christmas season, I was picked to be First Lady Nancy Reagan's "assistant" when she toured the Children's Hospital in Washington, D.C. My role? Santa Claus! Mrs. Reagan's secretary, Sheila Tate, knew that I had played Santa Claus for the National Park Service for the previous ten years, so I was "well suited" for the part. I was also the right weight!

I was the "mystery guest" dressed as Santa Claus at a party for the press corps that same year, and it was at that event that the First Lady served her famous Monkey Bread. It was a great hit, with "Santa" as well as the reporters, and Mrs. Reagan was kind enough to share her recipe with me for this book.

First Lady Nancy Reagan with Willard, our national Santa Claus. (Photo courtesy of Associated Press/Wide World Photos)

¾ ounce fresh yeast, or 1 package active dry yeast
1 to 1¼ cups milk
3 large eggs
3 tablespoons sugar
1 teaspoon salt

3½ cups all-purpose flour
¾ cup (1½ sticks) butter at room temperature
1 cup (2 sticks) butter, melted

In a bowl, mix the yeast with part of the milk until the yeast has dissolved. Add 2 of the eggs and beat. Mix in the dry ingredients. Then add the remaining milk a little at a time, mixing thoroughly. Cut in the ¾ cup butter until blended. Knead the dough; then let rise for 1 to 1½ hours, or until doubled in volume. Knead the dough again, and let rise for 40 minutes.

Roll the dough out on a floured board and shape into a log. Cut the log into 28 equal-size pieces. Shape each piece of dough into a ball and roll the balls in the melted butter. Butter and flour two 9-inch ring molds. Place 7 balls in the bottom of each mold, leaving space between them. Place the remaining balls on top, spacing them evenly. Let the dough rise in the molds. Brush the tops of the breads with the remaining egg. Bake in a preheated 375-degree oven for 15 minutes, or until golden brown.

★

Remember one of the basic Scott Principles of Fine Eating: New England cuisine rises to the mountaintops with ice cream and bakery goods.

This isn't the right spot for ice cream, but muffins I can give you—from Ed and Sue Ferrell's Down-East Village dining spot in Yarmouth, Maine.

☆ Blueberry Muffins ☆

2 cups all-purpose flour
¼ cup sugar
2 teaspoons baking powder
½ teaspoon salt
1 large egg, beaten

1 cup milk
¼ cup vegetable oil
2 teaspoons vanilla extract
1 to 1½ cups blueberries

Preheat the oven to 425 degrees. Combine all ingredients *except* the blueberries. Mix until moist; the batter will be lumpy. Stir in the blueberries. Spoon into greased muffin tins and bake for 20 minutes.
Makes 1 dozen.

★

One item you don't find on many of America's dining room tables these days is old-fashioned yeast bread. But that's not because there's anything wrong with the bread, it's just that many of those early American recipes have been lost. So here's one from the Wayside Inn in Middletown, Virginia, that you can include among your bread specialties.

☆ Old-Fashioned Yeast Bread ☆

2 packages active dry yeast
½ cup warm water (105 to 115
   degrees)
1 large egg, well beaten
1 cup milk
¼ cup sugar

2 tablespoons butter
1 tablespoon salt
5 to 6 cups sifted all-purpose
   flour
Melted butter

Dissolve the yeast in the warm water in a large mixing bowl; add the egg and stir well. Let stand for 10 minutes.

Combine the milk, sugar, 2 tablespoons butter, and salt in a small saucepan. Scald the milk mixture and cool to lukewarm; then add to the yeast mixture. Gradually stir in enough flour to make a soft dough that leaves side of bowl.

Turn out the dough onto a lightly floured surface and knead for 5 minutes, or until smooth and elastic. Shape into a ball and place in a greased bowl, turning to grease the top. Cover and let rise in a warm place (85 degrees) away from drafts for 1½ hours, or until doubled in volume.

Punch down the dough and knead for 1 minute. Shape into a ball and place in a greased bowl; cover and let rise for 1 hour, or until doubled in bulk.

Punch down the dough again and divide it into 3 equal portions. Shape each portion into a 6- by 3-inch loaf. Place the loaves in 3 greased 7- by 3½- by 2-inch loaf pans. Cover and let rise for 1 hour, or until doubled in volume. Bake in a preheated 325-degree oven for 20 minutes, or until the loaves sound hollow when tapped.

Remove the loaves from the pans, brush with melted butter, and cool on wire racks.
Makes 3 loaves.

★

The Normandie Farm Restaurant in Potomac, Maryland, is surrounded by fourteen acres of Potomac countryside. There are herb gardens and wildflowers just outside the restaurant's doorsteps, and the cuisine is a mixture of great American classics in the French tradition.

Although I was impressed by several of their dishes, the item that remains indelibly stamped on my memory—and also on my palate—is their popovers. I'd recommend them as a fantastic adjunct to any of the dishes which you may be preparing from this cookbook.

☆ Normandie Farm Popovers ☆

8 large eggs, beaten	1 teaspoon sugar
2 cups milk	2 cups all-purpose flour
1 teaspoon salt	Cooking oil

Mix the eggs, milk, salt, and sugar together in a large bowl. Add the flour and mix for 1 minute. Do not overmix!

Preheat the popover pan in a 400-degree oven with 1 tablespoon of cooking oil in each cup for 10 minutes. When hot, fill each cup three quarters full. Bake for 15 minutes. Lower the oven temperature to 350 degrees and bake for an additional 30 minutes. Be sure the popovers are cooked on the inside so they will not collapse when you take them out of the oven.

Makes 12 popovers.

★

Fans of bran will love this recipe for apple-bran muffins, which has made the rounds of many private New York City tables. The bran has a brisk, healthy texture, and the apples soften and sweeten it to make this item a real delicacy.

These muffins are wonderful for a formal dinner or gourmet meal, and just as appropriate as a between-meal snack or even a dessert for a group of schoolchildren.

☆ Sure-fire Apple-Bran Muffins ☆

1½ cups All-Bran cereal	3 teaspoons baking powder
1¼ cups lowfat milk	½ teaspoon salt
⅓ cup corn oil	1 apple, peeled, cored, and diced
1 large egg	2 to 3 handfuls raisins
1¼ cups all-purpose flour	1 teaspoon ground cinnamon, or
½ cup sugar	to taste

(Continued)

Preheat the oven to 400 degrees. Beat together the All-Bran, milk, corn oil, and egg with an electric mixer. In a separate bowl, mix the flour, sugar, baking powder, and salt together. Add the dry ingredients to the bran and stir until well mixed. Stir in the apple, raisins, and cinnamon. Pour into greased muffin tins and bake for 20 to 25 minutes. *Makes 12 muffins.*

★

My country upbringing has caused me to place a high premium on eating breakfast every morning. In fact, I love breakfast so much that I could easily keep eating it all the way up to lunchtime!

One thing I've discovered about a good breakfast, though, is that you have to deal straight-on with the delicate subject of the egg. The "incredible, edible egg" is how the industry extols it, and it truly is one of the most elegant and—in recent times—most maligned foods in the world.

Of course, there's no denying that hardening of the arteries, the major cause of the nation's heart attack epidemic, has been tied in directly to cholesterol in the blood. And it's hard to find any higher source of cholesterol than egg yolks.

But some people, like me, have no problem with cholesterol, no matter how many eggs they eat. Others may have a little problem; and still others have a *big* problem with cholesterol.

Now, I don't want to get into a health lecture here, because I'm hardly qualified to speak with any special expertise. But I certainly don't want to lead anyone down a primrose path to a heart attack. So, before you plunge into eggs in a big way, I would encourage you to determine, if you haven't already, how your body reacts to the consumption of eggs. Then make your own informed, personal decision about how you want to deal with these egg dishes.

★

The following recipe, from Nick's Fishmarket in Chicago, would be as appropriate for lunchtime as for breakfast. But, as I'm a big breakfast man, I prefer including this whopping Seafood Benedict as a candidate for the first meal of the day.

☆ Nick's Seafood Benedict ☆

¾ cup water
¼ cup dry white wine
1 bay leaf
⅓ pound bay scallops
⅓ pound shrimp, shelled and
 deveined
¼ pound mushrooms, sliced
BÉCHAMEL SAUCE
4 cups milk
½ cup (1 stick) butter
½ cup all-purpose flour
Pinch of ground nutmeg
Pinch of dried thyme
Salt and pepper to taste

HOLLANDAISE SAUCE
6 cups (12 sticks) butter
6 large egg yolks
Worcestershire sauce to taste
Tabasco sauce to taste
Lemon juice to taste
White pepper to taste

Water
4 large eggs, poached
2 English muffins, lightly
 toasted
2 black olives, sliced in half

To poach the seafood, bring the water, wine, and bay leaf to a boil. Add the scallops and shrimp and cook for 2 to 3 minutes, or until tender. Add the mushrooms and cook for 1 minute. Drain and remove the bay leaf. Set aside.

To prepare the béchamel sauce, heat the milk until it scalds. In another pan, melt the ½ cup of butter in a saucepan. Stirring the butter constantly, slowly add the flour and then the scalded milk. Add nutmeg, thyme, salt, and pepper. Cook over low heat for 3 to 5 minutes, or until the sauce thickens. Combine sauce with the seafood and mushrooms and cover to keep warm. (Yields 12 servings. The rest may be refrigerated for later use.)

To prepare the hollandaise sauce, melt the 6 cups of butter in a large saucepan. Skim the clear liquid off the top, discarding the milky substance at the bottom. In the top of a double boiler over simmering water, whip the egg yolks until stiff. Remove from the heat. Slowly add the clarified butter in a stream while whisking with a wire whisk until creamy and thick. Add the Worcestershire and Tabasco sauces, lemon juice, and white pepper. Cover to keep warm.

To assemble the dish, bring the water to a gentle boil in a small frying pan and poach eggs. The time will vary depending on one's preference for a softer or harder yolk. Place each egg on a toasted muffin half. Top first with the seafood mixture and then the hollandaise sauce. Garnish with a black olive slice.

Makes 4 servings.   147

★

Omelets are a meal in themselves, and in many respects they are the classic American kind of breakfast entrée. But I find some of the best have an interesting foreign twist.

These Austrian–American treats from Vienna '79 Restaurant in Manhattan should provide you with a pick-me-up, no matter how little sleep you got last night.

☆ Kaiserschmarren (Emperor's Trifle) ☆

½ cup all-purpose flour	Pinch of ground cinnamon
1 tablespoon milk	Pinch of salt
4 tablespoons granulated sugar	Clarified butter
4 large eggs, separated	2 tablespoons golden raisins
2 tablespoons rum	2 tablespoons butter
Grated rind of 1 lemon	Confectioner's sugar

Preheat the oven to 350 degrees. With an electric mixer, beat the flour, milk, and 1 tablespoon of the sugar to a smooth paste. Then beat in the egg yolks, rum, lemon rind, cinnamon, and salt.

In a separate bowl, beat the egg whites and 1 tablespoon of the sugar to a stiff meringue. Carefully fold the meringue into the other mixture.

Heat some clarified butter in two large ovenproof skillets. Pour the batter into the first skillet and fry on one side like an omelet. Add the raisins and flip the omelet into the second skillet. Transfer the skillet to the oven and bake for 10 minutes.

Remove the omelet from the skillet and, using 2 forks, tear the omelet into pieces. Return the torn omelet to the skillet; add the 2 tablespoons of butter and the remaining 2 tablespoons of granulated sugar. Heat through until caramelized.

Serve on 4 warm plates and sprinkle with confectioner's sugar. The Kaiserschmarren may be accompanied by the following compote.
Makes 4 servings.

☆ Cranberry Compote ☆

---

2 cups dry red wine   2 pounds cranberries, rinsed and
2 pounds sugar   drained

Combine the wine and sugar in a saucepan. Bring to a boil and simmer for 15 minutes. Add the cranberries and simmer for 10 minutes, stirring occasionally. Allow to cool, cover, and refrigerate until ready to serve.

★

Litchfield Park, the section of Phoenix, Arizona, where The Wigwam resort hotel is located, presents us with a fascinating piece of twentieth-century Americana.

The roots of Litchfield Park reach deep into the traditions of American capitalism. As the story goes, when the town was founded to provide a cotton supply for early Goodyear tires, the then-president of Goodyear, F. A. Seiberling, called on Paul W. Litchfield, then a lower executive.

"Litch," he said, "I doubt if this place ever will amount to much, so I think we will name it after you!"

Litchfield agreed, but even after he became chief executive officer of Goodyear a few years later, he never had reason to regret the community that had been named after him.

The cotton produced at Litchfield Park, an especially tough variety that enabled Goodyear tires to rise to the top rank of world tire production, helped firm up the tire and keep it firmly against the rim.

As the cotton business in Litchenfield grew in importance, Goodyear executives made frequent trips to the area, and they needed a place to stay. As a result, an "Organization House" was built to cater to their needs, and this structure eventually evolved into The Wigwam, one of the Southwest's most luxurious hotels.

(For a fuller account of this fascinating story, see Clyde E. Schetter, *Story of a Town—Litchfield Park,* published by The Litchfield Park Library Association.)

So the story of The Wigwam has strong, enduring ties to those events and developments that have made America a great economic power. Also, many of the foods served there, as tasty as they are, have become symbols of a thoroughly American culture.

Take the following recipe for corn fritters. Where else in the world could you find a dish that could better reflect the good, old-fashioned traditions of American country living?

It's no wonder that Clark D. Corbett, General Manager of The Wigwam, says that this dish is one of The Wigwam's "most asked for" recipes.

☆ Corn Fritters ☆

2½ cups all-purpose flour
¼ cup sugar
7 tablespoons baking powder
1½ tablespoons salt
12 large eggs, lightly beaten

2 12-ounce cans cream-style corn
1 12-ounce can whole-kernel corn, undrained
Clarified butter

With a hand mixer, beat the sifted dry ingredients into the combined egg and corn mixture.

Sauté in spoonfuls of clarified butter until puffed and golden on each side; drain on paper towels. Serve with hot maple syrup and grilled bacon.

Makes 6 servings.

★

When I'm on the road in New England, there's almost nothing that can "make my morning" like some melt-in-your-mouth Maine breakfast recipes. One that still gives me sweet dreams at night is a platter of blueberry pancakes, made with plump, juicy country blueberries, from the Down-East Village Restaurant.

☆ Blueberry Pancakes ☆

2 cups all-purpose flour
1 teaspoon baking soda
1¼ cups buttermilk
2 large eggs
¼ cup sugar

½ teaspoon salt
¼ cup vegetable oil
½ teaspoon vanilla extract
1 cup blueberries, washed and drained

Combine all the ingredients *except* the blueberries in a bowl and mix well. Stir in the blueberries. Cook on a hot griddle.

Makes 15 3-inch pancakes.

★

On other mornings, when I need an extra dose of strength and energy, I look for a breakfast which sticks to my ribs, even through a late lunchtime. The one that's made to order is this Birchermuesli from the Colonial Williamsburg.

☆ Birchermuesli ☆

1¼ cups uncooked oatmeal
1 cup heavy cream
1 pear, diced
8 red grapes, halved
2 tablespoons chopped nuts
¼ teaspoon *each* ground
   nutmeg and cinnamon

¾ cup milk
1 apple, diced
¼ cup raisins
8 white grapes, halved
1 teaspoon sugar
¼ cup honey

Combine all the ingredients in a large bowl; the mixture may be loose. If the mixture is too stiff, add more cream or milk. The mixture will stiffen up in the refrigerator.
Makes 6 to 8 servings.

From the Scott House
to Your House

O ne of the things I remember most vividly about when I was a kid during the 1940s was going to my grandfather's farm for a good old country meal. As I've already said in an earlier chapter, rationing of various goods started in this country at about the time the Second World War started. But on the farm, we didn't have any idea what rationing was when it came to food.

Some of the most delicious meals I've ever enjoyed came from the meat house behind the main farmhouse, where Grandfather cured some of the tastiest hams that the world has ever known! Those dinnertime delights impressed me as much as anything I've ever experienced. So on my own fifteen-acre farm down in Virginia, I've tried to recreate some of the festive atmosphere and fine eating that were part of our lives back in those days.

Now, in the next few pages, let me try to convey some of the succulent secrets that we've been enjoying for years down at the "Scott house." But I also want to mention one word of caution at the outset: These approaches to preparing and cooking meats and other foods are truly "country." That is, they were developed long before refrigeration and other scientific techniques became part of our lives. So I don't guarantee these procedures are going to coincide with every contemporary standard of food preparation. Certainly, they work for me; but for the sake of safety and culinary satisfaction, I'd suggest you check with your friendly neighborhood nutritionist, butcher, FDA representative, or other food expert *before* you try to use these procedures in your own home.

Willard hamming it up! (Photo courtesy of Diana H. Walker)

The Country Ham

Curing and cooking a country ham is as much an art form as a kitchen task. It all starts with a well-bred, prime pig and an old-fashioned meat house. And if you do it right, what finally ends up on the table in front of you is something close to heaven. Or as one old country wag has put it: "The definition of eternity is one country ham and two people."

The best place for curing hams is in the South Mid-Atlantic region, from Maryland down through North Carolina. In the old days, every farmer worth his ham hocks in that area had a meat house.

One of the reasons that this location is ideal for curing hams is the climate. The ideal temperature for butchering and curing in the grand old country style is somewhere between 35 and 45 degrees Fahrenheit. In that range, the meat stays cool and fresh, without freezing. (You can't cure frozen ham!)

Of course, the climate was especially important in the early days because they didn't have refrigeration. Now, with the proper equipment, you can cure hams anywhere. But if you want to do it the natural way, the South Mid-Atlantic region still reigns supreme.

My grandfather, who farmed in Maryland, raised his own pigs and then cured and cooked them with an old family recipe. I'm not quite that much of a purist: I buy the hams after the pigs have been slaughtered. But I still use his basic recipe, and that's part of what I want to share with you now.

I can still remember when I was five or six years old, standing there watching my six-foot-four-inch grandfather taking these huge hunks of ham, thirty to forty pounds each, and preparing them for the curing process. It's amazing how much I learned from my grandfather during the hog-killing time—which usually ran between Thanksgiving and Christmas. Butchering was never done until after Thanksgiving, mainly because the weather didn't turn cold enough until then. You might say I absorbed as much information about his techniques as he absorbed salt on his hands. And what I didn't pick up there, I learned from my uncle, who gave me a lot of pointers when I began to cure my own hams twenty years later.

Now, I buy my hams twenty-four hours after the animal has been butchered, so that the animal heat is out of the meat but it's still quite fresh. The process I use is known as "dry curing." This technique is different from an approach used in New England and some of the northern states, where the curing is done in a big vat of salt water.

I start out with a ham that weighs about 20 to 25 pounds (though this process will work just as easily with an ordinary family-sized ham of 8 to 12 pounds). I also get a box of Morton's Salt Cure.

In general, I just follow the directions on the box of Morton's Salt Cure. The package comes with a little pack of seasoning, and I usually mix some of that into the salt with a little sugar or pepper of my own, just to add a little additional zip to the taste. Then, I get a big mixing bowl out of our pantry, pour all the Salt Cure and the seasoning into it, and mix it around with my hands.

Then, I'm ready for the meat house. Basically, this is just a concrete building, with a place for a large, smooth board where I work on the meat. Also, there's a big pipe that's suspended inside it, which is used to hang the hams while they're curing. Finally, there's a hole or pit dug in the floor, where I build the fire for the smoking process.

Of course, most people don't have a real meat house, but a nice cool basement will do just as well. It's just important to make sure that it's fly-proof and mouse-proof.

First of all, I sprinkle the Salt Cure on the board and then set the ham, fat side down, on the board. And next comes the process of applying the Salt Cure.

The best way to apply the salt is just to *pat* the ham. *Never* rub the meat because that irritates it and makes it tough when you get ready to cut it. So, you gently cover every piece of that meat with the Salt Cure by patting it in; and it's also important to take your thumb and shove some of the Salt Cure down into those parts of the meat between the bones, so that as much of the salt as possible will get inside the ham and preserve it.

One big secret is to get the salt into the meat as fast as possible, so that all of the meat absorbs some salt within a twenty-four- to thirty-six-hour period. If I don't operate fairly quickly, my country ham may become a little "tainted," as the farmers say, around the bone. That just means that the salt cure didn't get to it fast enough, and part of the meat has gone bad.

One special "Scott technique" that I use in making the first applications of the salt is to put it on very lightly at first. If the directions say to put two applications on, I'll make it three—using a lot less the first time than the instructions may indicate. That way, the cook retains a lot more control over how much salt is put on.

Remember: A piece of meat will only take so much salt; each piece varies in its capacity to absorb. The biggest complaint you hear about country ham is, "It's too salty!" And, of course, if there's too much salt it not only *tastes* salty, but the salt also hardens the meat. On the other hand, just the right amount of salt can really make your mouth water. That's the main objective of these light initial applications.

So I put the salt on lightly, and watch the meat to see when that application gets absorbed. When I can no longer see any salt visible on the surface of the meat, it's time to put on another light application.

After the first few light "salt pattings," I'll let the meat sit in the meat house for three to four days. Then I'll go back and apply another light coating of salt.

The process goes on for about five weeks, with the ham lying there on the curing board. During that period, I'll check every few days to see whether the meat is still covered with a light coating of salt. Also, I want to be certain that it's not getting crusty. If the meat seems to need more salt, I'll pat a little on. If there's too much and it's getting crusty, I'll brush it off very lightly. I'll keep going back to repeat this process until my salt cure is used up.

Caution: It's important to follow the directions on the Salt Cure package to be sure that you use the right amount of salt for the size ham that you've chosen! In other words, if you have a 12-pound ham, you want to use enough salt for 12 pounds not a hundred. But even when you've used up the right amount of salt according to the instructions on the package, you continue to let the meat remain there on the board for a total period of five weeks, which should be measured from the time when you first began the curing process.

At the beginning of the last week, I make use of another old Scott family secret: I'll take the ham and turn it over. This way, the salt which was applied on the underside (the fat side) will have an opportunity to sink in more evenly than would be possible otherwise.

If I happen to run over the five-week period by a week or two, that's all right. But if I don't cure it long enough—say if I let the salt sink in only for about four weeks—I might have a little problem with the meat because the salt probably won't be distributed properly.

At any rate, after the meat has cured five to six weeks in the meat house, I take it out and wash it with cold water to get the excess salt off. My method of washing is to get some clear, natural water out of our springhouse, which is right next to the meat house. I'll pour the water in a big tub, place the ham in the water and take a scrub brush and rub it lightly over the meat.

Finally, I'll take a screwdriver, place it about 2 inches down the bone on the hock end, and make a hole through the bone. Then I'll take a piece of strong baling string and thread it through the hole. The loop that's formed is to hang the ham from the iron pipe that runs from wall to wall in the meat house.

What I'm doing at this point, of course, is "drip drying" the ham. That usually takes about two days, or however long it requires to get the excess water off the meat.

Then, it's time to build the fire for the smoking process.

Using hickory, apple, or any other hard, green wood, I'll get a fire started which burns slowly and gives off a nice, aromatic stream of smoke. The fire has to be really hot, but it's not necessary to have a great deal of smoke—a nice, fragrant wisp is all that's necessary.

Those operating without a regular meat house may buy a smoking device in many kitchen appliance stores, or they can make their own. One popular outdoor technique is to take a wooden barrel with the two ends knocked out, and place it one open end down on several cinder-blocks, right over the fire. Then, the cook places a pole at the top open end of the barrel, and hangs the ham from up there. But it's always important to keep the meat away from the flame. The idea is to get it smoked, but not burnt.

I usually smoke the ham for about three to four days and check the fire frequently to be sure that just the right amount of smoke is coming out. If the fire goes out or if there's too little smoke, the meat will fail to absorb sufficient smoky flavor. On the other hand, a huge, billowing bonfire can be just as bad for the final taste.

I'm always reminded of how the Indians used to smoke their fish and other game. As a general rule, they didn't use a meat house or any other enclosure. They'd just sit out over an open fire and smoke their meat right there. To be sure, they watched it closely, so that the smoke was always in contact with the meat, but they certainly didn't worry about smothering the meat in smoke.

After the fourth day of smoking, I'll go down and take the meat away from the fire. Then, I'll coat the meat with black pepper.

Next, I'll put some Borax on it. Yes, I really said Borax—the old-fashioned, "20-mule-team" kind of cleanser! But let me emphasize something again here: I'm just telling you the way *I* go through the curing process. I'm certainly not advising anyone to follow me every step of the way.

In any case, the reason for using the Borax is to keep flies off the meat while it's curing. So I'll pat the Borax all over the meat, and especially

157

at the hock end near the bone, because that part of the meat is quite vulnerable to flies.

Of course, I really don't get too worried if a few "skippers" (fly maggots) get into the meat. Maggots eat only rotted meat. So I figure they'll get rid of any parts of the ham that have inadvertently become "tainted" in the curing process. If I notice there are a few skippers in the meat, I'll let it sit out for a day in the light, and that's usually enough time to encourage them to crawl out.

But I'm getting ahead of myself: The curing process isn't finished yet. After I've covered the meat with Borax, I'll hang it up again from the string which is threaded through the hock.

The full time for the curing process is about nine months, but I may eat the ham anytime before that. Of course, the sooner I take it down and cut it, the more it will be like a fresh ham. For example, if our family eats it around Easter as an "Easter ham" the meat will be pink, but not fully cured. On the other hand, if we go for the full nine months, the meat will be a fully-cured red hue.

Now, let's suppose that the meat has been hanging up for the full nine months, which have passed so slowly I can hardly control myself. I've been thinking about it constantly—until now it's finally time to take it down and prepare it for the table.

First of all, I cut the hock end off with a knife. Then, I scrub the Borax off in cold water, put the meat in a big metal ham cooker (appropriate for the size of the ham), and let it soak overnight in the cold water. This way, every bit of the Borax and salt will be removed.

Then, I cook the cured ham the way an old railroad man taught me to do. As I've said, this is my own personal approach. There are many other ways of cooking ham. For example, to be absolutely sure any bugs, microbes, or whatever have been killed, plenty of experts think it best to cook it longer than I do.

Anyway, I boil the ham in a ham cooker at a "rollicking" (rolling) boil for 1 hour. That means the water has to be really bubbling up, and the liquid should be covering all the meat. Also, the cover should be on the ham cooker.

Then, when the hour is up, I'll pick up the ham cooker with the ham and water in it and put the whole thing on the floor in a corner. There, I'll wrap four or five blankets around the cooker to insulate it. This way, the ham continues to cook for 3 to 4 hours as the water cools down very, very slowly.

The reason for this slow-cooling technique is to keep the juices in the meat. You see, I'm going to cook it a final time a few days later, and if

I've taken steps to retain the juices at this point, my final product won't be as likely to become dried out.

The next morning, I'll take the ham out of the cooker and put it on a big baking sheet, with the fat side up. Then, I'll take a knife and "score" the ham.

This is done by cutting the fat on the outside of the ham into little cubes. I'll trace a line through the fat with the knife about every inch all the way around the ham. Then, I trace another set of lines every inch going lengthwise down the ham. I only allow the knife to cut about half an inch into the lean meat of the ham as I perform this procedure.

Finally, I'll pour some maple syrup rather generously over the top of the ham, put it into the oven, and bake it at about 250 degrees, for 45 minutes to 1 hour.

During the cooking process, the maple syrup crystallizes, and when the ham is "done," it's absolutely beautiful! A few cherries or orange slices can be placed on it before it goes on the table, just to dress it up.

Usually, if I start out this process with a 25-pound ham, I'll end up with about 20 pounds when I put it on the table. In other words, the ham will always lose weight during the curing and cooking process. This should be taken into account when trying to anticipate the number of people to feed.

Another thing I like about working with a ham is that nothing has to be wasted. I'll use the fat to cook beans or other foods. Also, some ham leftovers can be ground up and used to make "Smithfield ham spread."

★

But a country ham is only a little piece of the "hog heaven" pigs provide us with when we sit down to eat at the Scott house. Another favorite porcine pleasure is the country pork sausage.

☆ Country Pork Sausage ☆

24 pounds boneless pork (one third fat, two thirds lean)	8 tablespoons black pepper
	1 tablespoon cayenne pepper
9 tablespoons salt	1 tablespoon light brown sugar
9 tablespoons rubbed sage	

First, a preliminary note: I realized that we're talking about a lot of sausage here—24 pounds is enough to feed quite a party of people. If you want to make less, it's rather easy: Just reduce the amounts of the ingredients you use in proportion to the sausage.

It's important that the pork you choose for this dish be one third fat and two thirds lean because if it's all lean pork, the final result is going to be too hard to enjoy. The fat gives the sausage a great flavor and also makes it tender.

First, cut the pork up into bite-size cubes and put them into a mixing bowl. Then sprinkle all the remaining ingredients over the meat.

Note: If you have a problem eating salt, you can omit it from the food preparation at this stage. The reason for the salt, however, is to preserve the meat; so if you use less, you'll have to assume that the final sausage products won't remain fresh for as long a period. In fact, I'd advise you to consume unsalted sausage no later than the day after you prepare it. If you decide not to use salt, you can spice it up a little with a pinch of nutmeg and a pinch of ground-up cloves.

Then you work the ingredients into the meat with your hands and toss it around as you would a salad. Next you grind the meat up, either in an old-fashioned sausage grinder, such as I use at home, or in a newfangled contraption like the Cuisinart. When I use a grinder, by the way, I always put the meat through twice so that the sausage comes out finer.

Then I divide the ground pork into several large patties, about 4 or 5 pounds each. I'll wrap each of them up in wax paper and put them into the refrigerator or wrap them in plastic wrap and freeze them. *Caution:* Remember, if you haven't used salt, you really shouldn't keep the meat more than a day in the refrigerator, or it will go bad. But if you used the salt, the patties should stay fresh about a week.

It's a good idea to let these patties sit overnight, because then the seasoning has a chance to settle in—and that makes the sausage extra delicious. The next morning, I'll pull out one of those sausage loaves, slice off a few hamburger-size patties, and fry them slowly, as I would hamburgers.

I cook them in a medium rather than a hot frying pan, so that the sausage doesn't burn and it can get cooked thoroughly. It's a good idea to cook it so that it's really "well done." Then the sausage patties are ready to be served at your breakfast table.

By the way, another good reason for frying the sausage slowly is that you can collect plenty of good grease to use for cooking "puffs"—a Scott delicacy that I'd like to tell you about right now.

Makes 45 to 50 servings.

☆ Puffs ☆

Puffs have been a long-standing tradition in my family. We always had fresh, hot bread for dinner at my grandmother's house, and the leftovers from the yeast dough were perfect for our puffs recipe.

A puff, by the way, is a bread that literally explodes in the frying pan into a light, extremely tasty balloon. If you've ever eaten in an Indian restaurant, their poori bread is the closest thing I can think of to a puff.

The way I make a puff now is to get some Pillsbury Rolled Dough Mix and simply follow the instructions on the box for making the dough. When I have the dough all put together, I'll let it sit out for 2 to 3 hours; then I'll put it into a refrigerator until the next day. This way, some but not all the power of the yeast has been destroyed.

The next day, I'll dust a board with some flour and roll the dough into paper-thin pieces. Then I'll slice those pieces of dough into strips, about 3 inches long by 1½ inches wide.

The next step is to heat up some shortening or grease in a pan on the stove. When it gets hot, with a few bubbles of grease beginning to form in the pan, I'll toss a few strips of the dough into the pan. Just a few seconds after that dough hits the grease, it'll puff right up, like a balloon. With a pair of tongs, which I always keep nearby during this operation, I'll flip the puff over for a couple of seconds to brown it very lightly on the other side. Then I'll quickly take it out and put it on a serving platter lined with paper towels.

You have to really be nimble during this part of the process. If you wait too long, the puffs will get too dark and may even burn. But if you pull them out right at the right moment, they'll be a nice, light brown color.

Finally, to make the puffs extra tasty, I may open them at one end with a knife and then fill them full of jam or some other goody.

Putting It All Together: Willard's Favorite Country Breakfast

In my wildest fantasies, which I often live out in real life on our Virginia farm, I'll often take my country ham, country sausages, and puffs and combine them with several other delicacies to produce what I regard as the perfect breakfast.

At the Scott house, a July morning is the best time for this event.

Fruit is always a part of this breakfast, so I'll spend a little time picking peaches when they first come in during July. At about the same time, I can find some wild blueberries and raspberries. I have some cultivated fruit that I'll include as well.

And don't forget the applesauce! We make applesauce from the apples on our trees, and I may also fry a couple of apples. Then, I'll throw in some grits that I buy down at the local country store.

Finally, it's not past me to have both a piece of sausage *and* some ham dish that I'll make from the country ham.

For example, I may take the cured hock end of the ham, clean off the Borax, and without boiling the meat, slice off a few thin pieces for frying.

Then I'll throw the ham into a frying pan and begin to fry it very, very slowly. The frying process can be helped along by putting in a tablespoon of water at the bottom of the pan. I'll constantly turn each slice of ham just to be sure that it cooks all the way through and doesn't burn.

If I fry it slowly enough, the ham fat begins to cover the bottom of the pan, and this sets me up for the next tasty step: I'll take the ham out after I've fried it for 15 to 18 minutes and put it on some paper where it can drain. But I'll leave the ham fat in the pan and pour in about half a cup of black coffee, to make "redeye gravy."

Then, as this gravy is bubbling along, I'll break a couple of eggs over it and cook them until they're just the hardness I prefer. As they cook, I'll usually take a spoon and spread a little of the redeye gravy over the eggs, so that it forms a delicious film.

Finally, after I take out the eggs, I'll put the redeye gravy in a bowl and place it on the table, so that it can be poured over the grits.

So what do we finally have when we Scotts sit down at our breakfast table, with the strong morning sun streaming through the windows? Some might say that it's a breakfast that would "gag a moose." But as for me, I can't think of anything that's much closer to heaven.

Sometimes I'll just sit there for a few moments, surveying the magnificent breakfast table tableau and inhaling those wonderful, mouthwatering aromas. At that moment, I know I've put it all together: The country ham, duly represented by those fried slices of ham hock. The grits, crowned by their redeye gravy. The poached-fried eggs, also permeated by the gravy flavor. The puffs, uplifted by the applesauce. The fried apples. The fresh peaches, blueberries, and raspberries.

Can you imagine anything more wonderful? I can't.

☆ ☆ ☆

Glossary

Angostura bitters: A common mixer for drinks which comes from the bark of South American trees.

Béchamel sauce: A generic white sauce usually used with fish; see the recipe on page 147.

Blanch: To boil or steam something in order to remove its skin, whiten it, or prepare it for freezing or canning.

Bok Choy: A Chinese cabbage.

Bouquet garni: An assortment of herbs tied together, usually used in preparing soups.

Brown veal sauce: A version of brown sauce (or espagnole) made from *veal* stock, thickened with flour which has been browned in fat, seasoned to taste.

Caramelize: To change (usually sugar) into caramel, by heating.

Cayenne pepper: A very hot powder made by drying and then grinding up hot peppers.

Charlotte: A dessert with infinite varieties. All have in common a bread layer and a filling layer, as follows: bread, cake, or cookies line a dish. On top of that layer is placed some filling (custard, mousse, whipped cream, fruit, etc.).

Chiffonade: A term for finely chopped or shredded vegetables when they're used to make soups or salad dressings.

Clarified butter: Melted and strained or skimmed; purified.

Cold smoke: Smoking at a temperature between 70 and 90 degrees F.

Collard greens: Smooth-leaved kale.

Compote: Fruits cooked in a sugar syrup. Also, they have retained their shape, so they aren't broken down and haven't fallen apart.

Glossary

Crawfish sauce (bisque): A thick cream soup made with crawfish.

Cream (as a verb): To stir, beat, or blend into a creamy consistency.

Curing salt: Salt or salt product used for curing meat.

Demi-glace (Sauce): A version of brown (espagnole) sauce that has been reduced, strained, and seasoned, often made with dry wine.

Escargots: Snails.

Farmer cheese: A pressed cheese of whole milk or partly skimmed milk, made on farms.

Fatback: What it sounds like—a strip of *fat* from the *back* of a hog.

Feta cheese: A white cheese made from sheep's or goat's milk, cured in salt water.

Filé powder: Powder made from young sassafras leaves, used in soups and stews.

Fish fumet: For our purposes, fish *stock*.

Glace: A glaze, a smooth glossy finish, or any frozen dessert.

Hollandaise sauce: A common sauce with many varieties, generally including egg yolks, butter, and vinegar or lemon juice. See recipe pages 87 and 147.

Julienne: Cut into long, thin strips, usually a way of preparing raw vegetables or fruits.

Juniper berries: Blue, berry-like fruit from a juniper bush or tree.

Kale: A curly-leafed cabbage; the smooth-leaved type is called collard greens.

Kohlrabi: A vegetable of the cabbage family that has a turnip-shaped stem.

Kosher salt: Coarse-grained sea salt naturally high in minerals and iodine.

Liaison: A smooth combination of elements, such as cream and egg yolks, usually used as a thickening agent.

Macerate: To soften or separate a substance into its component parts by soaking it in water or another fluid.

Parma ham: Ham from Parma, Italy.

Parsnip(s): The root of a European herb that grows wild in North America but is poisonous in its wild state. It is cultivated for table use. Usually used in the plural.

Pâté: A spread or paste made of ground and seasoned meat, poultry, or fish.

Personal seasoning: Means salt and pepper, but think twice before you throw it in because we all use more of both than is good for us.

Red currants: Red fruit from the currant often used for jams or jellies. There are also black and white currants.

Reduce: Boiling away excess liquid, thus concentrating flavor and decreasing volume, especially in a gravy or sauce.

Reserve: To set aside and save for future use.

Rolling or "rollicking" boil: A high, bubbling boil.

Rose water: A watery solution made from fresh roses that have been distilled with water or steam.

Roux, roux blanc: A flour and fat mixture used to thicken soups and sauces; always cooked, sometimes browned.

Scald: For milk: to heat *almost* to boiling without letting it boil; for other ingredients: usually to boil or steam for the purpose of loosening skin or feathers.

Score: Long furrows, scratches, or incisions made into a vegetable with the tines of a fork, often for its entire length (e.g., cucumber). A checkerboard pattern cut by a knife into the outside surface of a piece of meat.

Separate: To break a mixture down into its parts. For eggs: to isolate the "whites" from the "yolks."

Set: To allow a preparation to harden or stiffen into a set shape, if it's a dessert.

Shallot(s): An herb resembling an onion used for seasoning

Sit: Place something off to one side so that it will rise (yeast), dry, or cool.

Springform pan: A resuable pan which has an upright rim that detaches from the bottom of the pan, thus making it easier to get the contents out. Usually made for desserts, especially cheesecakes.

Stock: A liquid base for soups and stews made by simmering chicken or fish or beef or even vegetables, sometimes with spices. After simmering, everything is removed except the liquid; then, the liquid is strained. Usually stock is made in advance of need and set aside for future use.

Sturgeon: Any of the edible freshwater or saltwater fishes which produce the fish-egg delicacy caviar.

Truffle(s): Check your context! This is either the edible fruit of a subterranean fungi, or a rich, whipped-chocolate-with-butter confection.

Vanilla sugar: Results from having a vanilla bean sit in sugar for a while so the sugar can pick up some of its flavor. See page 36.

Venison: Deer meat.

Vinaigrette: A common sauce or dressing, usually a combination of oil, vinegar, onions, parsley, and various herbs. See the recipe on page 127.

Whisk in: To mix or fluff one ingredient or product into another, using a wire whisk.

Whole pickling spices: The spices used in a salt or vinegar solution for pickling and preserving fish, meat, vegetables, fruit, etc.

☆ ☆ ☆

Willard's
Best in America

BEST "KNOCKWURST"	Chicago Airport
BEST HAMBURGER	Jackson Hole, New York City
BEST PIZZA	Gino's, Chicago
BEST ICE CREAM	Anywhere in Boston (Largest Consumer of Ice Cream); also East India in Orlando, Florida
BEST OVERALL OYSTERS AND CRABS	From Chesapeake Bay; also Wintzell's, Mobile, Alabama
BEST BLUEFISH	Legal Sea Food, Boston, Massachusetts
BEST CHILI	Frank Tolbert's, Dallas, Texas
BEST MEXICAN FOOD	Tee Pee Mexican Food Restaurant, Phoenix, Arizona; La Fuente, Tucson, Arizona; and La Fogata, San Antonio, Texas
BEST NAVY BEAN SOUP	Senate Cafeteria, Washington, D.C.
BEST BAKERY	Shuman's, Alexandria, Virginia
BEST CHOCOLATE CANDY	Marshall Field's, Chicago
BEST DELICATESSEN	Kaplan's, New York City
BEST VEAL CHOP	The Giraffe, New York City
BEST STEAK	Little Abner's, Tucson, Arizona
BEST BROILED CHICKEN	Post House, New York City

167

BEST BARBECUE	McClard's, Hot Springs, Arkansas; Various Places in Little Rock, Arkansas
BEST CHEESECAKE	Junior's, Brooklyn, New York
BEST VEGETABLE PLATTER	Woods, New York City
BEST CATFISH	Peabody Hotel, Memphis, Tennessee
BEST ROAST BEEF	Bubble Room, Captiva Island, Florida
BEST JALAPEÑO MUFFIN	K-Paul's, New Orleans, Louisiana
BEST BREAD PUDDING	Arnaud's, New Orleans, Louisiana
BEST STONE CRABS	Joe's, Miami Beach, Florida
BEST BLUE CRABS	Phillip's, Ocean City, Maryland
BEST SUBMARINE (HOAGY)	Lee's, Philadelphia, Pennsylvania
BEST PASTA	Il Monello, New York City
BEST CHOCOLATE CAKE	Four Seasons, New York City
BEST APPLE PIE	Norske Nook, Osseo, Wisconsin
BEST CHINESE FOOD	Leeann Chin, Minneapolis, Minnesota
BEST BRUNCH	Ranchos los Palmas, Palm Springs, California (a Marriott Hotel)
BEST AMERICAN RED WINES	Wittiken Vineyards, Little Rock, Arkansas
BEST CAFÉ	Café du Monde, New Orleans, Louisiana (Beignets and New Orleans-style Chicory Coffee)
BEST SOURDOUGH BREAD	Bogatz, San Francisco, California
BEST SALMON	Coco's, Portland, Oregon
BEST AMERICAN SMOKED SALMON	The Airport, San Francisco, California
BEST SHRIMP DISH	The Sea Captain's House, Myrtle Beach, South Carolina
BEST GUMBO	K-Paul's, New Orleans, Louisiana
BIGGEST DESSERT CAKE	RJ's on Rodeo Drive, Beverly Hills, California
BEST CHICKEN SOUP	Kaplan's, New York City

BEST CHICKEN SOUP HOME RECIPE	Esther Brandice, New York City
BEST CLAM CHOWDER	Harvard Club's Friday Meal, New York City
BIGGEST AND TASTIEST SANDWICH	Carnegie Deli, New York City
BEST SALAMI	Katz's Delicatessen, New York City
BEST JELLY CAKE	Shuman's Bakery, Alexandria, Virginia
BEST PEANUTS	Portales, New Mexico
BEST ICE CREAM ON A STICK	The Dove Bar
BEST DISTILLED SPIRITS	Jack Daniels
BEST CHEESE STEAK SANDWICH	Pat's Steaks, Philadelphia, Pennsylvania
BEST FRIED CHICKEN	The Loveless Motel, Nashville, Tennessee

Send your own "Best" or favorite recipe to:
Willard Scott
NBC
30 Rockefeller Plaza
New York, NY 10036

☆ ☆ ☆

Featured Restaurants

(Including Contact Person)

Ms. Narcisse S. Cadgene
Bis! Restaurant
1626 York Avenue
New York, NY 10028

Katie and Jamie Farquharson
The Bubble Room
P.O. Box 458
Captiva Island, FL 33924

George and Jeannine Sterckx
Captiva Inn
P.O. Box 445
Captiva Island, FL 33924

Executive Chef John P. Turner
Chadwick's
South Seas Plantation Road
Captiva Island, FL 33924

Ms. Victoria Fabiano
The Charcoal Grill Steak House
9903 West Brown Deer Road
Milwaukee, WI 53224

Mr. Alfred W. Jones, Jr.
The Cloister Hotel
P.O. Box 351
Sea Island, GA 31561

Brian and Loretta Jillson
Coachstop Restaurant
P.O. Box 1036
Middleburg, VA 22117

Ms. Susan Bruno
Colonial Williamsburg
    Foundation
P.O. Box C
Williamsburg, VA 23187

Ed and Sue Ferrell
Down-East Village Restaurant/
    Motel
P.O. Box 178, U.S. Rte. 1
Yarmouth, ME 04096-0178

Mr. and Mrs. Robert R. Clifford
The Gourmet House
P.O. Box 130
Bismarck, ND 58502

171

Mr. Rodney G. Stoner
Executive Food Director
The Greenbrier
Station A
White Sulphur Springs, WV
    24986

Mr. Ray Colvin, General Manager
Jake's Famous Crawfish
   Restaurant
401 S.W. Twelfth
Portland, OR 97205

Mr. Irwin Sawitz
Joe's Stone Crab Restaurant
227 Biscayne Street
Miami Beach, FL 33139

Jo Willa G. Lopez, President
The Junior League of the City of
   New York
130 East 80th Street
New York, NY 10021

Mr. Paul Prudhomme
K-Paul's Louisiana Kitchen
406 Chartres Street, Apt. 2
New Orleans, Louisiana 70130

Ms. Hope Davis
La Fuente
1749 North Miracle Mile
Tucson, AZ 85705

Mr. Roger S. Berkowitz
Legal Sea Foods Inc.
33 Everett Street
Allston, MA 02134

Mr. Willy Krause
Le Pèrigord Park
575 Park Avenue
New York, NY 10021

Max and Lanie Pincus, Owners
London Chop House
155 West Congress Street
Detroit, MI 48224

Ms. Kimberly Palazzo
Mader's Restaurant
1037 North Third Street
Milwaukee, WI 53203

Chef Nino Azzara
The Mad Hatter
6460 Sanibel-Captiva Road
Sanibel Island, FL 33957

Mr. Victor Mayeron
The Mucky Duck
P.O. Box 1060
Captiva, FL 33924

Mr. Nick Nickolas, Owner
Nick's Fish Market
First National Bank Building
First National Plaza
Chicago, IL 60603

Mr. Stephen Longley
Normandie Farm
10710 Falls Road
Potomac, MD 20854

Ms. Peggy Ritter
The Pioneer Club
One Lakeside Plaza
Lake Charles, LA 70601

Mr. Herbert S. Traub
The Pirates' House
20 East Broad Street
Savannah, GA 31401

Mr. Prince C. Bowens, III
Prince's Place (Mrs. Frances'
  Kitchen)
1111 Dunbar Street
Myrtle Beach, SC 29577

Mr. David Brittain
Sea Captain's House at Ocean
  Front and Sea Captain's House
  at Murrel's Inlet
P.O. Box 218
Myrtle Beach, SC 29577

Mr. Tom Fournaris
The Stock Yard Inn
1147 Lititz Pike
Lancaster, PA 17601

Mr. Tony Duran
Tee Pee Mexican Food Restaurant
4144 East Indian School Road
Phoenix, AZ 85018

Ms. Charlotta Wiles Carper,
  Manager
Timmy's Nook
Captiva Road
Captiva Island, FL 33924

Mr. Peter Grunauer
Vienna '79
35 East 60th Street
New York, NY 10022

Ms. Anne Smalley
Wayside Inn
7783 Maine Street
Middletown, VA 22645

Mr. Clark D. Corbett
Vice President and General
  Manager
The Wigwam
P.O. Box 278
Litchfield Park, AZ 85340

Mr. Tom Burke, Sr.
Wintzell's Oyster House
605 Dolphin Street
Mobile, AL 36602

Mr. Ronald P. Sharky
Woods Restaurant
718 Madison Avenue
New York, NY 10021

☆ ☆ ☆

Index

Index